Penguin Special

The Penguin Guide to

Tony Lynes was born in 1929 and qualified as a
chartered accountant in 1951. He worked in Malta for
four years and from 1956 to 1958 studied social
administration at the London School of Economics
where he became involved with Labour policy-making on
social security. In 1966, after a year at the Ministry of
Pensions, he became full-time secretary of the Child
Poverty Action Group and from 1969 to 1970 a full-time
consultant on social security with Oxfordshire
Children's Department. Tony Lynes is at present
researching on the Unemployment Assistance Board,
helping with social security advice services, writing on
social security for various periodicals and running a
class on social security tribunals at the L.S.E. He has
lectured at American universities and took part in the
1967 conference on children's allowances organized by
the Citizens' Committee for Children of New York. His
publications include *French Pensions* (1967) and
Labour's Pension Plan (1969).

Tony Lynes

THE PENGUIN GUIDE
TO SUPPLEMENTARY
BENEFITS

Supplementary Benefits, the
Family Income Supplement
and the Appeals Tribunal

Penguin Books

Penguin Books Ltd, Harmondsworth,
Middlesex, England
Penguin Books Inc., 7110 Ambassador Road,
Baltimore, Maryland 21207, U.S.A.
Penguin Books Australia Ltd, Ringwood,
Victoria, Australia

First published 1972

Copyright © Tony Lynes, 1972

Made and printed in Great Britain by
Richard Clay (The Chaucer Press) Ltd, Bungay, Suffolk
Set in Monotype Garamond

CONTENTS

CHAPTER 3.
HOW BENEFIT IS CALCULATED – (2) RESOURCES 63

CHAPTER 4.
ABOVE THE MINIMUM 72

7

ACKNOWLEDGEMENTS

This book could not have been written without the generous help of officials of the Department of Health and Social Security who read and commented on my drafts, answered innumerable queries and suggested many amendments. In most cases I have followed their advice, but not in all, and they are in no way responsible for any factual errors that remain.

Similar help on particular aspects was given by the Department of Education and Science, the Department of Employment, the Home Office, the General and Municipal Workers' Union, the Institute of Housing Managers, International Social Service of Great Britain, the National Association for Mental Health, the National Council for the Unmarried Mother and her Child, the National Union of Mineworkers, and the National Union of Students, and by Mr Simon Hillyard, Mr A. P. Mapplebeck, Mr J. Pannell and the indefatigable Mrs Helen Slater, to all of whom I am most grateful. A special word of thanks is due to Mrs Iris Goodacre, Mrs Audrey Harvey and Mr Charles Marshall, each of whom read my first draft and suggested numerous improvements.

Finally I would like to thank all those who, during the past fourteen years, as claimants, social workers, officers of the Supplementary Benefits Commission, and students have taught me most of what I know about this esoteric and, until recently, neglected subject.

Tony Lynes

Ivy Cottage, Lower Heyford,
Oxford

Summer 1972

INTRODUCTION

This book is about two parts of the complicated network of social security benefits in Great Britain – supplementary benefit and the family income supplement. Its purpose is to inform rather than to reform; to advise rather than to criticize. It is intended to help both those who are entitled to benefits and their professional and voluntary advisers.

Every effort has been made to ensure that the information given is up to date at the time of writing. Changes made in the family income supplement scheme in April 1972 and those made in the supplementary benefit scheme in October 1972 have been taken into account. But the ways in which the Supplementary Benefits Commission uses its very wide discretionary powers are constantly changing and no guide of this kind can be completely up to date. Moreover, the basic supplementary benefit scales are now adjusted annually and most of the figures given in the text and in the appendixes will have to be revised towards the end of 1973 at the latest. There is no simple answer to this problem, but readers may care to use the blank column in Appendix 1 to insert the 1973 amendments to the supplementary benefit scale.

Supplementary benefit is the latest name for what used to be called national assistance – it was renamed in 1966. It is sometimes described as the safety net of the social security system, since its object is to ensure that everybody receives a minimum income which is at least enough to live on. This object is not always achieved, not only because the amount of benefit paid is sometimes inadequate, but also because some people with very low incomes cannot get supplementary benefit at all. The most important group that is excluded consists of families in which the breadwinner is in full-time work but cannot earn enough to provide a reasonable standard of living for the family. Supplementary benefit is normally paid only to those who are unable to work full-time, either because of age, sickness, family responsibilities or other personal factors, or because suitable jobs are not available. The family income supplement scheme was introduced in 1971 as a first step towards filling this gap. Only those in full-time work (and therefore unable to claim supplementary benefit) and with at least one child can claim a family income supplement. The two schemes thus complement each other, and the same family may be entitled to family income supplement when the head of the family is working and to supplementary benefit when he or she is out of work.

SOCIAL SECURITY IN BRITAIN

Before describing the supplementary benefit and family income supplement schemes in detail, it may be helpful to give a brief summary of the broader framework of social security benefits of which they are a part.

The main form of State provision for those whose earnings are interrupted or terminated, and for their dependants, is the national insurance scheme. The benefits provided by the scheme are summarized in Table 1.

TABLE 1

Unemployment benefit	(a) Flat-rate benefit payable after three days and continuing for up to a year;
	(b) A supplement based on the individual's previous earnings, payable after two weeks and continuing for up to six months.
Sickness benefit	(a) Flat-rate benefit payable after three days for as long as incapacity for work continues or until replaced by invalidity pension;

    (b) A supplement based on the individual's previous earnings, payable after two weeks and continuing for up to six months.

Invalidity benefit

    (a) Flat-rate invalidity pension replacing sickness benefit after twenty-eight weeks and payable for as long as incapacity for work continues;

    (b) Invalidity allowance, varying with age at which incapacity began, provided this was more than five years before retirement age; payable as long as incapacity continues.

Attendance allowance

Flat-rate allowance for severely disabled people needing attention or supervision from another person.

Maternity benefits

    (a) Lump sum maternity grant, payable before birth of child, whether the mother has been in paid work or not;

    (b) Flat-rate maternity allowance payable for eighteen weeks, starting eleven weeks before baby is due, if the mother has worked and paid full national insurance contributions.

Retirement pension

    (a) Flat-rate pension paid on retirement at or after age 60 for women, 65 for men (may be reduced if earnings exceed £9·50, but not after age 65 for women, 70 for men);

    (b) Graduated pension, based on earnings-related contributions;

    (c) Increments earned by deferring retirement;

    (d) Addition for pensioners over 80.

Old persons' pension

Flat-rate pension at a lower rate for those over 80 who would not otherwise get this amount of pension.

Widows' benefits

    (a) Flat-rate widow's allowance payable for first twenty-six weeks of widowhood;

    (b) Widow's supplementary allowance based on husband's earnings, paid in addition to widow's allowance if husband died before qualifying for retirement pension;

    (c) Widowed mother's allowance payable when widow's allowance ceases, for as long as the widow has a son or daughter under 19 living with her or dependent on her;

                    (d) Widow's pension payable *either* when widow's allowance ceases, if widow was over 40 on husband's death and is not entitled to widowed mother's allowance, *or* when widowed mother's allowance ceases if then over 40 (widow's pension is reduced if the widow is under 50 when husband dies or widowed mother's allowance ceases).

Guardian's allowance	Payable to a person providing a home for a child whose parents are both dead, or where one parent is dead and the other cannot be traced or is serving a long prison sentence.
Child's special allowance	Payable to a divorced woman on her former husband's death, for a child maintained by him while he was alive.
Death grant	Lump sum payable on death.

Since all these benefits except the attendance allowance and the old persons' pension are subject to contribution conditions, some people do not get them because they have not paid (or been credited with) the right number and kind of contributions. For instance, a man who has not contributed as either an employed or a self-employed person will not qualify for sickness benefit; and if he has contributed but has less than fifty contributions paid or credited in the last contribution year he may qualify but his benefit will be paid at a reduced rate.

There is a separate and more generous industrial injuries scheme covering claims by employees arising from accidents at work and industrial diseases. As well as giving higher basic rates of benefit for time off work, it provides a disablement benefit based on the degree of disablement and payable even if the disabled person goes back to work, with additional allowances for constant attendance, exceptionally severe disablement and hospital treatment, and an unemployability supplement for those who are permanently incapable of work. In cases of relatively slight disability, disablement benefit may be paid in a lump sum rather than as a weekly pension. A widow whose husband died as a result of an industrial accident or disease receives a more generous pension than if death was due to other causes.

Rather similar to the industrial injuries scheme, in that it provides benefits related to the degree of disablement with additional allowances for constant attendance etc., is the war pensions scheme. Although new awards are comparatively few, there are still many people drawing war pensions that were awarded in the past.

Both the main national insurance scheme and the special schemes described above include provision for dependants. For example, an unemployed man with a wife and three children to support will get a flat-rate national insurance benefit made up as in Table 2. The allowance of £4·15 for a

TABLE 2

Self	£6·75
Wife	4·15
First child	2·10
Second child	1·20
Third child	1·10
	£15·30

dependent wife is not paid if she is working and earning more than this amount, after deducting income tax, national insurance contributions, fares and any other expenses connected with her job. The reason for the varying allowances for children is that they take into account the family allowances which the family will normally receive whether the father is in work or not: 90p for the second child and £1·00 for each subsequent child. Thus, while the father is unemployed, the total allowances paid for each child amount to £2·10.

Higher children's allowances are paid for the children of widows and invalidity or retirement pensioners – £3·30 per child, including family allowances. The dependent wife of an invalidity or retirement pensioner is also treated more generously in that she can earn up to £9·50 per week without any reduction of her husband's pension. Widows are allowed to earn whatever they can without any reduction of their national insurance benefits.

THE SUPPLEMENTARY BENEFIT SCHEME

The national insurance, industrial injuries and war pensions schemes together provide for a very wide variety of circumstances which might otherwise cause financial hardship. Why, then, should it be necessary to have yet another scheme from which, in November 1971, benefits were being paid to 2,909,000 people to meet their own needs and those of 1,655,000 dependants – altogether over 4½ million people?

There are two reasons. The first is that where national insurance and similar benefits are available they are often inadequate, even when added to the claimant's other resources. One of the main functions of supplementary benefit, therefore, is to top up the benefits payable under the national insurance scheme. Over 2·1 million of the 2·9 million people drawing supplementary benefit in November 1971 were also in receipt of national insurance benefits. Of these, 1,816,000 were retirement pensioners (mostly women) and widows over retirement age. The other 340,000 were unemployed, sick, disabled, or widows under 60. The predominance of older people in these figures is due to the fact that they tend to remain in need of benefit for much longer periods than most younger claimants. The vast majority of the claims for benefit received in the course of the year were from claimants under pension age, but most of them, if they were awarded benefit at all, had ceased to receive it by November and are therefore not included in the 990,000 younger claimants who were then actually drawing benefit.

In most cases, therefore, supplementary benefit is truly supplementary in that it supplements other benefits to which the claimant is entitled. But there is a smaller number of claimants – about 750,000 in November 1971 – who for a variety of reasons do not qualify for national insurance benefits, and who are in many cases wholly or mainly dependent on supplementary benefit for their weekly income. They include unmarried mothers, separated wives, unemployed men who have exhausted their entitlement to insurance benefit or are disqualified from receiving it, strikers, single women looking after elderly relatives, people suffering from long-term or congenital disabilities, either physical or mental, who have never worked and thus do not qualify for insurance benefits, men staying at home to care for children while their wives are absent or ill, certain limited categories of students with dependants, and a wide variety of people who, for whatever reason, have been unable to fulfil the conditions for claiming insurance benefits.

The supplementary benefit scheme was created by the Ministry of Social Security Act, 1966. The Act lays down the basic rules of the scheme and the original rates of benefit. These rates have been amended subsequently by regulations approved by Parliament. Other regulations set out more detailed rules regarding certain aspects of the scheme. Some important changes, mainly affecting strikers and those regarded as voluntarily unemployed, were made by the Social Security Act, 1971.[1]

The Acts and regulations provide the legal basis of the scheme. To understand how it operates in practice, however, it is not enough to look at this broad legal framework. Equally important are the discretionary powers of the Supplementary Benefits Commission, the body appointed under the 1966 Act to decide 'whether any person is entitled to benefit and the amount of any benefit'. These discretionary powers enable the Commission to depart from the basic rules in a very large number of individual cases. The Commission's discretion is not unlimited but it is extremely wide, and this guide is very largely about the ways in which it is exercised.

The Commission itself has produced an extremely useful booklet, the *Supplementary Benefits Handbook*, setting out 'the broad lines along which the Commission exercises its dis-

1. The Acts and regulations currently in force are published in *The Law relating to Supplementary Benefits and Family Income Supplements* (H.M. Stationery Office, 1972, £2·50). An additional charge is made for loose-leaf supplements keeping the volume up to date.

cretionary powers in day to day administration'. The first edition appeared in 1970 and provided far more information than had previously been publicly available about the Commission's policies on a wide range of questions. A second edition was published in April 1971, and quotations from the *Handbook* in this guide are taken from this revised edition, the latest available at the time of writing (a third edition is expected towards the end of 1972). But the *Handbook*, useful though it is, is not a complete guide to the scheme, for two reasons. First, it leaves out a good deal of detailed information without which it is often impossible to tell whether the treatment of a particular case is in accordance with the Commission's normal policy or not. Such omissions were no doubt dictated by a laudable desire to keep both the length of the *Handbook* and its price within reasonable bounds. Whatever the reason, however, the fact remains that there are many questions which the *Handbook* does not answer. Secondly, while the *Handbook* explains the Commission's official policies, it does not necessarily explain what happens in individual cases, which often depends on the judgement of the local officer dealing with the case. Similar cases may be dealt with differently by different local social security offices, or even by different officers attached to the same office. Moreover, although the Commission's officers receive detailed instructions, in a series of voluminous 'codes' (notably the 'A Code'), dealing with the principles to be applied in different types of cases and combinations of circumstances, individual officers may not always act in accordance with their instructions. This may be due to ignorance or confusion – there is not always time to consult the relevant code before making a decision, and the instructions are complex and sometimes difficult to understand. Or it may be that the instructions on a particular point run counter to the customary procedure which has been followed over the years. Or again, the officer may feel that his own judgement on the merits (or demerits) of the case is more valid than the policy laid down by the Commission.

This guide, therefore, does not only explain the legal framework of the scheme and the official policies of the Commission regarding the use of its discretionary powers, going into more detail than the *Supplementary Benefits Handbook* on a number of points. It also attempts to show how the scheme operates at the level where the vast majority of individual decisions are made – the level of the local social security office – and some of the ways in which day-to-day administration at the local level may differ from the carefully devised policies of the Commission.

THE FAMILY INCOME SUPPLEMENT SCHEME

The Family Income Supplements Act, 1970, extended the functions of the Supplementary Benefits Commission by making it responsible for deciding 'any question as to the right to or the amount of a family income supplement'. The scheme was introduced as a result of widespread concern about the existence of a considerable number of families with incomes below the minimum level provided by the supplementary benefit scheme, but who were not allowed to receive supplementary benefit because the breadwinner of the family was in full-time work. It permits the incomes of such families, provided that they have at least one child, to be raised by half the amount by which they fall short of a 'prescribed amount' laid down in the Act and amended by subsequent regulations.[1] In other words, while the supplementary benefit scheme aims at filling the whole of the gap between the claimant's other resources and his minimum needs, the family income supplement (generally known as FIS) fills only half the gap, and sometimes less than half, since the maximum supplement payable is £5 a week. The first payments of FIS were made in August 1971 and by the end of the year 66,000 families were benefiting from the scheme – about half the number believed to be entitled.

Unlike supplementary benefit, FIS is based on clear rules of entitlement, leaving little room for the use of discretion. It is

1. See footnote on page 19.

therefore much easier to describe and to understand than the supplementary benefit scheme. Hence it occupies only part of one chapter of this guide (Chapter 8).

THE RIGHT OF APPEAL

Both the Ministry of Social Security Act and the Family Income Supplements Act give claimants the right to appeal against the Commission's decisions to an independent tribunal. Chapter 9 describes how the tribunals work and explains how to make the best use of them. One of the objects of this book is to encourage claimants to use the appeal machinery when they have good grounds for doing so, and to provide them with the information they need in order to judge whether an appeal is justified or not. A far more important object, however, is to give claimants a fuller understanding of their rights and of the Commission's policies, so that they can meet the officers of the Commission on a more equal footing and obtain the benefits to which they are entitled without the need to resort to the appeal tribunal. It is not more appeals that are needed but more satisfied claimants.

Chapter One

GETTING SUPPLEMENTARY BENEFIT

THE RIGHT TO BENEFIT

Supplementary benefit is a legal right – subject to a number of qualifications. Section 4(1) of the Ministry of Social Security Act starts as follows: 'Every person in Great Britain of or over the age of sixteen whose resources are insufficient to meet his requirements shall be entitled, subject to the provisions of this Act, to benefit . . .' But the right to benefit is neither as clear-cut nor as automatic as the word 'entitled' might suggest.

The term 'supplementary benefit' covers three different kinds of benefit:

(a) *Supplementary pensions* for people over pension age (65 for men, 60 for women);
(b) *Supplementary allowances* for people under pension age;
(c) Single payments to meet *exceptional needs*.

Only the first of these involves anything like an automatic legal right. The Commission may decide that a supplementary pension should be increased to take account of any special needs, but it cannot reduce it below the basic level calculated in accordance with the regulations. Even the calculation of this basic level, however, may involve an element of discretion with regard to the amount to be allowed for rent. Anything above the minimum, such as extra allowances for fuel, laundry or domestic help, is given on an entirely discretionary basis, not as a right. It is true that section 3(1) of the Ministry of Social Security Act directs the Commission to 'exercise the functions conferred on them by this Act in such manner as shall best promote the welfare of persons affected by the exercise thereof'. From this it could be argued that the Commission has a duty to make reasonable use of its discretionary powers, and it is possible that, in an extreme case, legal action could be taken to compel it to do so. But such cases rarely, if ever, occur. Normally, the only remedy available to a claimant who is dissatisfied with the way in which the Commission has exercised its discretion is an appeal to the local tribunal, which has the same discretionary powers as the Commission itself.

While pensioners have a legal right to a minimum level of income, only slightly modified by discretion with regard to rent, persons under pension age claiming a supplementary allowance may have their benefit reduced below the normal minimum level if there are 'exceptional circumstances', or it may even be withheld altogether, subject to the right of appeal. The discretionary power to reduce or withhold a supplementary allowance is used mainly where the claimant is suspected of being 'workshy' (see pages 138–45), but it may be used to justify a refusal to pay benefit at the normal rate in other circumstances, provided that they are 'exceptional'.

The third type of benefit – a single payment to meet an exceptional need – is always discretionary, whether the claimant is over or under pension age, and whether he is already receiving benefit on a weekly basis or not. Some kinds of need are met more or less automatically (e.g. payments to a woman on supplementary benefit to visit her husband in prison), in which case they become virtually a right. In effect, the Commission decides in advance how its discretionary powers are to be used in a whole class of cases. But 'rights' of this sort are never absolute, because it is always open to the Commission to decide that the general rule it has laid down does not fit the facts of a particular case.

There is another reason why the concept of rights as normally understood in English law does not apply to supplementary benefits. Although there is a right of appeal to a local tribunal, there is usually no possibility of a further appeal to a higher tribunal, commissioner or court. As a result, there is no established body of case law laid down by the courts, which would have to be followed in later cases. The fact that one case was dealt with in a particular way does not entitle other people to similar treatment if the Commission decides to treat them differently. Whether this is a bad thing is a matter of judgement. The Commission's deputy chairman, Professor Titmuss, has argued that 'legalization' of the system would make it less flexible and more mystifying to the average claimant.[1] It is certainly true that, if the Commission's decisions were circumscribed by a massive body of precedents, it would be much more difficult for claimants to make use of the appeal machinery without skilled legal assistance.

From all this it will be clear that supplementary benefit is not a legal right in the same sense as, for instance, national insurance benefits, for which both the rates and the qualifying conditions are laid down in considerable detail. Even in national insurance, the judgement of the insurance officer plays an important part – in deciding, for example, whether an unemployed man 'has neglected to avail himself of a reasonable opportunity of suitable employment'; but if he is not satisfied with the decision, he can appeal not only to a local tribunal but from there to the National Insurance Commissioner, whose decisions constitute legal precedents. There is thus a useful body of case law on the meaning of 'a reasonable opportunity of suitable employment', which at least ensures that subsequent decisions on this point are based on consistent and ascertainable principles. And nowhere in the national insurance scheme are officials given the wide discretionary powers conferred on the Commission by the Ministry of Social Security Act.

It would be wrong, however, to suggest that a supplementary benefit claimant under pension age has no rights. The policies of the Commission set out in the unpublished 'codes' and summarized in the *Handbook* may not be legally enforceable, but they do represent a code of practice which must be observed by individual officers unless there are

1. Richard M. Titmuss, 'Welfare "rights", law and discretion', *Political Quarterly*, April 1971, pages 113–32.

genuine reasons for departing from it. This is, admittedly, a limited safeguard, since there is seldom much difficulty in showing that there are 'exceptional circumstances' in a particular case; but it does at least provide a standard against which the actions of officials can be checked.

It must always be remembered that, just as the claimant has no legally enforceable rights in the areas covered by the Commission's discretionary powers, similarly the Commission's policy regarding the use of those powers has no legal force. Not only does each claimant have the right to dispute the application of the general policy to the circumstances of his case. More important, he has the right to take the disputed decision to an appeal tribunal which is in no way bound by the Commission's policy. The tribunal thus has far greater freedom than the Commission's officers, who, at least in theory, are bound by the instructions handed down to them from headquarters. The powers of the tribunals are discussed more fully in Chapter 9, but throughout this guide frequent reference will be made to the right of appeal, especially where the Commission's stated policy appears questionable.

WHO CAN CLAIM BENEFIT?

The three main conditions for receiving supplementary benefit are laid down in section 4(1) of the Ministry of Social Security Act, quoted at the beginning of this chapter: the claimant must be in Great Britain, he (or she) must be aged 16 or over, and his resources must be insufficient to meet his requirements – that is to say, he must be in need. If he has a wife and/or dependent children living with him, their requirements and resources are added to his for this purpose. The way in which resources and requirements are worked out is explained in Chapters 2–8. Before turning to the detailed calculations, however, we must first note some important categories of people who, even if they satisfy the three conditions of section 4(1), are still not eligible for benefit.

Full-time workers

People in full-time paid work cannot receive supplementary benefit, with the following exceptions:

(a) In 'an urgent case';

(b) During the first fifteen days after starting or restarting work;

(c) Where a disabled person is self-employed but his earning power is substantially lower than that of other people in the same occupation;

(d) In the case of a married couple, the fact that the wife is in full-time work need not prevent the husband from claiming benefit if their combined resources are not sufficient to meet their requirements.

A person in full-time work who is not eligible for supplementary benefit but whose income is low may qualify for a family income supplement. The circumstances in which persons in full-time work may receive supplementary benefit or FIS are explained fully in Chapter 8.

Strikers and persons laid off because of a strike

A person directly involved, however unwillingly, in a strike or trade dispute cannot claim benefit for himself, but he can claim for his wife and children. See pages 125–30.

Wives

A married woman living with her husband cannot claim benefit in her own right, though her needs will be included with his if he is eligible to claim. The same rule applies to a woman living with a man as his wife although not in fact married to him, unless there are 'exceptional circumstances'. See pages 154–61.

Young people staying on at school

A boy or girl over 16 but still at school cannot claim benefit unless there are exceptional circumstances or the need is urgent. Payment of benefit in such cases is very rare, since help is normally obtainable from the education department or the social services department of the local authority.

People able to work but not 'signing on'

A person under retirement age who is not prevented from doing paid work by illness, the care of children or other circumstances will usually have to register for work at the employment exchange as a condition of receiving benefit. Section 11 of the Act, which gives the Commission the power to impose this condition, does not state in what types of case it should or should not be imposed, except that it *cannot* be applied to supplementary pensioners. The Commission's policy on this point is set out in paragraphs 7 and 8 of the *Handbook*:

7. Claimants who are *not* required to register include:
   (1) people who are incapable of work – based on medical evidence of incapacity;
   (2) women who have their dependent children under 16 living with them;
   (3) blind persons who have not been accustomed to working outside the home.

8. For certain other groups of people the requirement to register may be waived or registration for part-time work only may be required, depending on all the circumstances of the case. These include:
   (1) people required at home to care for sick relatives;
   (2) women widowed in late middle life with no experience in the employment field and where there is evidence of some ill-health;
   (3) people on training or other educational courses where *either* they would be unlikely to work without the course *or* some event during the course makes their education grant or training allowance insufficient to maintain their dependants.

The requirement to register for work may affect not only the decision as to whether benefit is payable but also the amount of benefit, since the amount of part-time earnings that can be disregarded in assessing the resources of the claimant is smaller for those to whom the condition applies than for other claimants. Those required to register for work are also not eligible for the 'long-term addition' of 60p. (See page 36). Even if there is little prospect of full-time work being available, therefore, some loss of benefit may result. There is a right of appeal against the requirement to register and it should be used in any case where the requirement seems unreasonable or unnecessary.

Claimants, especially unsupported mothers, sometimes report that, although they have not been *required* to register for work as a condition of receiving benefit, an officer has suggested that they *ought* to look for a job. Such suggestions may be made with the best of motives, but they are apt to be interpreted by the claimant as either a threat of withdrawal of benefit or an accusation of 'scrounging', or both. It should be understood that, once the Commission has decided not to impose the requirement to register, it is for the claimant to decide whether voluntarily to seek employment or not.

HOW TO MAKE A CLAIM

The procedure for claiming supplementary benefit is extremely simple. The claim must be made in writing. Claim forms (SP1 for persons over pension age, S1 for those under pension age other than the unemployed) can be obtained from the post office, which will also supply on request an envelope addressed to the local social security office – it doesn't even need a stamp. All that need be written on the form is the claimant's name and address. There is a space for him to indicate if his need is urgent. It is advisable to claim as soon as the need arises, as benefit will normally be paid only from the date of the claim.

For unemployed people, the procedure is slightly different. Claim form B1 can be obtained only at the employment exchange, which will forward it to the social security office unless the claimant prefers to do so himself.

There is normally no need for the claimant to call at the social security office, and it is usually best not to do so since it can sometimes entail a long wait in rather unpleasant surroundings. Within a few days of sending in the claim form, he will be visited at home by a social security officer, whose job it is to obtain all the information needed in order to decide how much benefit (if any) is payable. The officer will normally send a note saying on what day he proposes to call, but this may not arrive until the morning of the day of the visit; so it is advisable to stay at home until the first post arrives. Notification of the amount of benefit due, together with the first payment, should arrive within a day or two of the home visit. This timetable is subject to a good deal of variation in practice. If the claimant has stated on the claim form that his need is urgent, a visit should follow within two or three days. Otherwise it may take a week, and considerably longer delays may occur if pressure of work in the local office is particularly heavy.

If a visit to the local office is necessary, it is best to avoid going on a Friday, which is usually the busiest day of the week; Tuesday and Wednesday are generally the quietest days. And it is important to go armed with all the documents that are likely to be needed in order to deal with the claim: the rent book or other evidence of rent, mortgage payments or lodging charge, family allowance book, bank books or statements, evidence of the last wages received and of any part-time earnings and national insurance benefits in payment; in short, any papers that will help to show the claimant's exact financial situation or substantiate the grounds for his claim (e.g. medical certificates). Without these, payment may be refused until a home visit has been made. Provided that *all* the necessary evidence is produced, it should be possible for the full amount of benefit to be put into payment at once, and the claimant should receive a giro order the following day. In practice what usually happens is that a provisional payment is made, which is less than the full entitlement. The balance is paid after a home visit has taken place, but it is important to ensure that this actually happens. If benefit is needed only for a fairly short time, the home visit may not take place and the claimant may have to write to the social security office to ensure that any underpayment of benefit is made good. Whether a full payment or a provisional payment is made, the claimant will not be told on the spot how much he can expect to receive but will have to wait until the money arrives through the post. The reason for this is to cut down waiting time in the office, but it can cause a good deal of anxiety, especially if the claimant is uncertain whether he will receive any benefit at all.

In very exceptional cases, an immediate payment may be made across the counter (usually in the form of a giro order which can be cashed at the post office). According to the *Handbook*, this is done 'if a person is genuinely in such urgent need that he cannot reasonably be expected to wait for payment until the following day'. Local offices are extremely reluctant to make such payments, and it is advisable to get a social worker or other person known to the office manager to telephone him and explain the circumstances in advance. Even then, success cannot be guaranteed, and it may be wiser to look for other sources of immediate help rather than waste several hours in an attempt to extract a small sum of money from the social security office.

One type of case in which reluctance to make payments across the counter causes difficulties is that of the man or woman without a fixed address. The Commission cannot assess his normal weekly benefit entitlement until he finds permanent accommodation. If he can show that he has a promise of suitable lodgings, the local office may be willing to make a payment of the amount of rent needed to secure the accommodation. Otherwise, he will probably be given a voucher entitling him to a bed and full or partial board at a lodging house or similar establishment if such accommodation is available in the area. Once in this situation, it can be very difficult to escape from it. To obtain normal accommodation usually involves producing at least a week's rent, which is clearly impossible for a man receiving only a small amount of pocket money while the rest of his weekly benefit is paid in the form of vouchers. The Commission, however, is unwilling to make cash payments to claimants with no fixed address, since in the past it was not unknown for men to travel from one local office to another, drawing benefit at each.

It is possible to appeal against the award of benefit in the form of a voucher for goods and services rather than cash, or against the value of the goods and services provided (it could reasonably be argued, for instance, that if the Commission insists on issuing vouchers in order to prevent fraud, it could at least enable the claimant to obtain decent accommodation rather than treating him as a tramp). But the appeal machinery may not be very useful because of the delays involved. In the two or three weeks that it takes, as a minimum, to get an appeal heard, the claimant may well have found work or solved the problem in some other way. Even if he has not, two or three weeks in a lodging house is a long time!

PREVENTING DOUBLE PAYMENTS

It often happens that a person who has received supplementary benefit for a particular period later receives other benefits in respect of the same period which, had they been paid earlier, would have reduced the amount of supplementary benefit payable. To prevent the overpayment which would result if the second benefit were to be paid in full, section 16(1) of the Ministry of Social Security Act provides that the amount of supplementary benefit already paid for the same period can be deducted from it. The benefits from which such deductions can be made include most national insurance benefits (but not maternity grant or death grant), industrial injury benefits, family allowances and family income supplement.

Example: Owing to delay in payment of unemployment benefit, a claimant receives the whole of his income for three weeks in the form of supplementary benefit at the rate of £8 per week. He is told later that he was entitled to unemployment benefit at £6·75 per week for four weeks and two days (£29·25 in all), including the three weeks for which supplementary benefit was paid. But for the delay, his supplementary benefit would have been £6·75 per week less, or £20·25 less for the three weeks. This sum is deducted from the unemployment benefit due, leaving a balance payable of £9.

PAYMENT IN KIND OR TO A THIRD PARTY

Under section 14 of the Ministry of Social Security Act, the Commission can provide goods and services instead of cash where, because of exceptional circumstances, this seems the best way of meeting a person's needs. In addition to the practice of issuing lodging vouchers (see page 31), this power is used mainly in emergencies, e.g. after a fire or flood. Section 14(2) provides that, when meeting 'sudden and urgent need' in this way, the Commission 'may dispense with inquiry into resources or other circumstances and with compliance with any regulations made under this Act'.

Benefit may be paid to someone other than the claimant, under section 17(3), either at the claimant's request (to which the Commission is not bound to agree) or to protect his own or his dependants' interests. Rent can be paid direct to the landlord under this provision. See page 55.

LATE CLAIMS

Benefit cannot normally be paid for a period before the claim reaches the social security office. The Commission may, however, treat a claim as having been made on an earlier date if it is satisfied that there are exceptional circumstances justifying such action (regulation 6(3) of the Supplementary Benefit (Claims and Payments) Regulations 1966 (Statutory Instruments, 1966, No. 1067)). If there is a good reason for delay in making a claim, therefore, the Commission should be asked to pay arrears of benefit.

Chapter 2

HOW BENEFIT IS CALCULATED
(1) REQUIREMENTS

The normal way of working out how much supplementary benefit is payable is quite simple, but there are a number of special rules for particular types of case. In the normal case, the benefit payable is the amount by which the claimant's resources fall short of his requirements; and the method of calculating requirements and resources is laid down in schedule 2 of the Ministry of Social Security Act, though as usual the Act leaves a good deal to the discretion of the Commission.

A household consisting of a married couple (or an unmarried couple living together as man and wife) and their dependent children are treated as a single unit, and benefit to meet their combined needs must be claimed by the man. If there are other people living in the household – whether as lodgers, visitors or members of the family (including children no longer dependent on the claimant) – their requirements and resources will not be taken into account, except to the extent that they are assumed to pay a share of the rent. See pages 40–42.

A 'dependent' child is one who has not left school or, occasionally, a low-paid apprentice. A young person aged 16 or over who has left school and is looking for a job or for some reason is unable to work is entitled to claim benefit in his own right. This is particularly important for a family with a handicapped child over 16 who is unable to work. He is entitled to an income in his own right, whether his parents are rich or poor. At the other end of the scale, an old person living with grown-up children or other relatives can claim benefit in

34

his own right, even if the relatives are able and willing to support him – though in practice a pensioner living with relatives and drawing a retirement pension at the standard rate (£6·75 from October 1972) will not qualify for a supplementary pension unless he has special needs.

THE SUPPLEMENTARY BENEFIT SCALE

Supplementary benefit is intended to provide an income that people can live on – not just enough to keep them alive but an income related to the normal standards of the community as a whole. The government decides from time to time – normally once a year – just how much is needed to achieve this aim, and the resulting figures are laid down in regulations which have to be approved by Parliament. Just how the figures are arrived at is a closely guarded secret. They are certainly not based on scientific estimates of subsistence needs. Perhaps the most important factor taken into account is the relationship of supplementary benefit payments to the incomes of low-paid workers which provide, in effect, an upper limit to the government's generosity, since it is generally felt to be wrong that anybody should be as well off out of work as in work (the wage-stop rule ensures that they are not *better* off out of work; see pages 109–25). In practice, the annual increases are generally about enough to restore the relationship between benefit and wages, thus giving supplementary benefit recipients a proportionate share in the rising standards of the working population.

Just as we do not know how the amounts of money allowed for the total requirements of claimants and their dependants are arrived at, similarly we are not told how much is included in the total figures for the various elements in the household budget – food, clothing, fuel, and so on. The only exception is rent, which is dealt with separately. (See pages 37–57.) Other needs are lumped together in a global figure, leaving the claimant free to spend his income as he wishes.

The supplementary benefit scale, showing the amounts

allowed for normal requirements other than rent, is set out in Appendix 1. The rates shown are those which came into force on 2 October 1972. The examples given in Appendix 2 show how the total requirements of a claimant are calculated from these figures. The requirements of supplementary pensioners and other long-term recipients are increased by a 'long-term addition' of 60p a week (85p if the claimant or his wife is over 80). The amount of the long-term addition is the same for a married couple as for a single person. All supplementary *pensioners* qualify for the addition, other than lodgers and those in hospital or old people's homes – but a married couple will be classed as supplementary pensioners only if the *husband* is over pension age. Persons under pension age receiving a supplementary *allowance* get the long-term addition only if they have drawn benefit for two years or more and have not been required to register for work in the past two years – i.e. the long-term unemployed do not qualify for the addition. On a strict interpretation of the Act, if a person under pension age temporarily ceases to qualify for the long-term addition, either because he stops drawing benefit or because for a time he is required to register at the employment exchange, he cannot requalify for another two years. This could obviously be unfair, so in practice the Commission uses its discretionary powers to restore the addition at once if the interruption is not longer than thirteen weeks. Similarly, in deciding whether the addition should be awarded in the first place, interruptions of up to thirteen weeks in the two-year qualifying period are ignored. A further relaxation of the rules is made in the case of a widow drawing a supplementary allowance, who is allowed to count a period during which her husband was drawing benefit immediately before his death in her two-year qualifying period.

We shall have more to say about the long-term addition when we come to discuss the additional allowances that can be given to meet specific needs. See pages 82–4.

One other item in the scale of requirements in Appendix 1 calls for some explanation – the allowance of £5·40 or £3·60 for 'attendance requirements'. This represents the amount of the national insurance attendance allowance for severely disabled people introduced in 1971. Originally the attendance allowance was payable at a single rate (£4·80, increased to £5·40 in October 1972) to those in need of attention or supervision both by day and by night. The lower rate, £3·60, for those whose need arises either by day or by night but not both, will come into operation by stages between June 1973 and December 1974, starting with those of working age and then taking in children and, finally, the elderly. In introducing this new benefit, the government wished to ensure that supplementary benefit claimants who qualified for it should receive it in addition to their basic supplementary benefit entitlement, as a right, rather than as a discretionary addition awarded by the Supplementary Benefits Commission on grounds of exceptional circumstances. Accordingly, it was decided that an amount equal to the attendance allowance should automatically be included in the assessment of the claimant's requirements.

It should be noted that the allowance for attendance requirements in the supplementary benefit scale applies only in those cases where either the claimant himself or one of his dependants is entitled to the national insurance attendance allowance. In other cases where paid attendance is necessary, the cost can be taken into account by the Commission in assessing the claimant's requirements in the same way as any other exceptional need (see Chapter 4). Similarly, where the attendance allowance is in payment but does not cover the full cost of attendance, a further addition should be made to the claimant's requirements to cover the difference.

THE TREATMENT OF RENT

Because of the wide variations in housing costs, rent is not included in the scale of requirements given in Appendix 1. In calculating the claimant's total requirements, therefore, an allowance for rent must usually be added to the scale rates.

How this allowance is calculated depends on whether the claimant is a tenant, owns his own home, or is a member of somebody else's household. The various possibilities are explained below.

Householders paying rent

In the case of a claimant who is the tenant of rented accommodation, the amount allowed for rent is normally the full amount of rent and rates paid by him, worked out on a weekly basis, or as much of it as is considered reasonable in the circumstances. Most tenants are eligible for a rent rebate or rent allowance under the Housing Finance Act, 1972 (or the Housing (Financial Provisions) (Scotland) Act, 1972), if their income is low enough. These Acts lay down a model rent rebate scheme which, apart from minor variations, all local authorities must operate for their council tenants from October 1972, and a similar scheme of rent allowances for tenants of private landlords and housing associations commencing in January 1973.[1] If a tenant who has already been granted a rent rebate or rent allowance claims supplementary benefit, the rent rebate or allowance continues at the same rate for the first eight weeks during which supplementary benefit is paid, and the net rent, after deducting the rebate or allowance, is taken into account by the Commission in assessing the claimant's requirements for supplementary benefit purposes, provided that it is considered reasonable (the circumstances in which a rent may be considered unreasonable are explained below). If the tenant has not yet claimed a rent rebate or allowance, the Commission will calculate his requirements for the first eight weeks on the basis of the full rent – or as much of it as is reasonable.

Whether the tenant is already getting a rent rebate/allowance or not, if he is still in receipt of supplementary benefit after

1. Furnished tenancies will not be covered initially by the rent allowance scheme. At the time of writing, however, the Government is considering the possibility of including them at a later stage.

eight weeks and the tenancy falls within the provisions of the scheme, the local authority will award a rebate or allowance calculated according to special rules applicable to supplementary benefit claimants (but note that these rules do not apply to claimants whose benefit is limited by the 'wage stop'; their rent rebate/allowance is calculated in the same way as that of a person in full-time work, and they do not have to wait eight weeks before it commences; see page 124. This will normally have the effect of reducing the net rent to 40 per cent of the 'fair' rent (40 per cent of the 'standard' rent in the case of council tenants in Scotland) assessed by the appropriate authority, or to £1 if this is more than 40 per cent of the 'fair' rent; but the rebate/allowance will be reduced if there are non-dependent members of the household or if it would otherwise exceed the maximum permitted by the Acts (£8 in the Greater London area and £6·50 elsewhere). If rents in the area are exceptionally high, the Secretary of State may authorize the granting of higher rebates and allowances than would be given under the model scheme; but this power does not apply to Scotland.

The local authority is automatically informed by the social security office when a tenant claims supplementary benefit, so that the appropriate rebate or allowance can be awarded after the first eight weeks without any need for the claimant to make an application. In most cases, the precise method of calculating the rebate/allowance is not of great importance to the claimant, since his supplementary benefit will normally be adjusted to take account of any alteration in his net rent, leaving him neither better nor worse off on balance. In some cases, however, the granting or increasing of a rebate or allowance reduces the tenant's total requirements to a level at which he no longer qualifies for supplementary benefit at all. In that event, he stands to gain from any further increase in the rebate/allowance and it is worth checking that the calculation has been carried out correctly.

To arrive at the amount of weekly rent taken into account by the Commission in assessing the claimant's requirements for supplementary benefit purposes, a number of other adjustments may be necessary. If the rent is payable monthly, it must be multiplied by three and divided by thirteen to arrive at a weekly figure. Some local authorities divide the yearly rent by 50 or 48, giving their tenants either two or four 'rent-free' weeks in the year. Where this happens the total rent payable in the course of the year must be divided by 52 to arrive at the real weekly rent. Rates, if not included in the rent, must also be worked out on a weekly basis.

If the rent includes payments for heating, lighting, or other services which the Commission regards as being covered by the supplementary benefit scale, an appropriate deduction is made to arrive at the net rent. No deduction is made merely because furniture is provided, unless the landlord not only provides such items as crockery and linen but renews them when necessary – and there are not many landlords who do that. Where they do, a deduction of 5p per week is made. In the much more usual type of case where the rent covers the cost of electricity, gas or other fuel for heating, lighting, hot water or cooking, an estimate is made of the amount the claimant would be likely to spend on the items covered if he had to provide them for himself, and this amount is deducted. The precise amount of the deduction therefore depends on the circumstances of the particular case. For heating alone, including hot water, £1·20 a week is deducted. If lighting and fuel for cooking are also supplied, the deduction is £1·35. If only partial heating is provided, or the actual cost to the landlord (e.g. for heating a small room) is obviously less than £1·20, a smaller deduction is made. There is, of course, no need for estimated adjustments of this kind if the rent includes a definite amount for, say, central heating, since that amount will automatically be deducted. Where a fixed charge of this kind for heating is more than £1·20 a week, it is worth asking for a special addition to meet the extra cost. See page 75.

If there are people living in the household other than the claimant and his wife and dependent children, the amount allowed for rent may be reduced by their share of the rent (or, as the Ministry of Social Security Act puts it, 'such part of the net rent as is reasonably attributable to that other person'). No adjustment should be made in respect of a person who is merely on a short visit – e.g. a grown-up son or daughter spending a holiday with the claimant. In other cases, the amount of rent attributable to non-dependent members of the household clearly depends on the amount of space and privacy enjoyed by them. The Commission applies a rough and ready formula, counting each person aged 16 or over as one unit and each child under 16 as a half unit, and apportioning the rent (before deducting any rebate or allowance) accordingly.

Example: Mr and Mrs P. live with their son William in a council house. Mr P. is unemployed and claiming supplementary benefit. William is in full-time work. The 'fair' rent of the house is £5 a week and the rates are £1 a week. They get a rent rebate of £1·50, reducing the weekly rent and rates to £4·50. For supplementary benefit purposes, William's share of the rent is taken as a third of £6, or £2 a week. The amount allowed for rent and rates in calculating Mr P.'s requirements is therefore £4·50 less £2, or £2·50 per week. If Mr and Mrs P. also had two children under 16, William's share of the rent would be only a quarter of £6, or £1·50, since the household would then comprise four units (three adults and two children).

In most cases, this formula produces reasonable results – but not always. There are three points to bear in mind. First, if there is an obvious discrepancy between the proportion of rent attributed to the non-dependant and the proportionate value of the accommodation occupied by him, the Commission can be asked to adopt a different basis for splitting the rent. Refusal to do so would provide grounds for an appeal. Secondly, the Act merely says that the rent allowance '*may* be reduced by an amount *not exceeding* such part of the net rent as is reasonably attributable to that other person' (schedule 2, paragraph 13(2) – my italics). The reduction may therefore be less than the non-dependant's reasonable share of the rent. It is the Commission's policy to make a smaller reduction if the non-dependent person obviously cannot afford to pay his full share. No reduction at all is made if the non-dependant is under 16. If he is 16 or over, the amount of rent attributed to him is reduced, if necessary, to an amount which will leave him with a margin of at least £1 over the scale rates for him and his dependants (if any). If he is under 21, an alternative method of calculating his assumed contribution to the rent is used if it produces a lower figure: he is allowed to keep the first £4 a week of his earnings and half the remainder, the other half being regarded as available as his contribution towards the rent.

Example: A claimant lives with his wife and daughter aged 17 in privately rented accommodation. The weekly rent is £6 including rates (he has not claimed a rent allowance from the local authority), and the proportion attributed to the daughter would normally be one third or £2. The daughter's net earnings are £7 a week. After deducting the scale rate for a non-householder aged 17 (£4·05) and allowing a margin of £1, only £1·95 remains available for rent. But the alternative method, deducting the first £4 of earnings and half the remainder (£1·50), leaves only £1·50 for rent. The amount of rent to be taken into account in assessing the claimant's requirements is therefore £6 less £1·50, or £4·50.

It may happen that the non-dependant is in receipt of supplementary benefit in his own right. In that case, the amount he will be assumed to be contributing towards the rent will be the amount allowed for rent in calculating his benefit – normally 70p.

The third point to be noted is that, if the claimant or his wife is blind, the Act does not permit any reduction in the amount allowed for rent where there are non-dependants.

If part of the accommodation is sub-let, a further reduction must be made in respect of the proceeds of sub-letting. In calculating the proceeds, expenses connected with sub-letting must be deducted from the rent received. Fixed sums are allowed for wear and tear and for any services provided, such as electric light and heating. These allowances are due for revision at the time of writing, and the revised figures should be broadly similar to the amounts deducted from the claimant's rent where services are provided by the landlord (see page 40). If the actual expenses incurred are higher than the amounts allowed, an increased allowance can be requested. It is important to note, however, that the claimant is not allowed to retain any profit or compensation for the inconvenience of sub-letting part of his home. The only circumstances in which sub-letting will result in any financial advantage are where the Commission would otherwise refuse to include the full net rent in the claimant's requirements on the grounds that it is unreasonable, or where the claimant is repaying a mortgage. (See page 51.) A claimant who is not already sub-letting should therefore consider the consequences carefully before doing so.

Unreasonable rents

The Ministry of Social Security Act provides, in paragraph 13 of schedule 2, that in assessing the requirements of a house-holder the Commission must add the weekly net rent (including rates etc.) or 'such part of that amount as is reasonable in the circumstances'. In the great majority of cases, the full weekly rent is allowed, but there are exceptions.

The April 1971 edition of the *Handbook* explains that

in deciding whether a rent is reasonable or not local officers ask themselves:

(1) whether the rent is reasonable for the accommodation provided;

(2) whether the accommodation is reasonable for the claimant.

It then lists the following principles to be observed in considering the second of these questions – whether the accommodation is reasonable for the claimant:

(1) a claimant is not expected to lower his standard of accommodation unless that standard is clearly higher than is provided, say, in average Local Authority accommodation in the neighbourhood;

(2) if the accommodation is expensive and unnecessarily large, it would be contrary to the public interest if supplementary benefit were paid to enable him to remain there indefinitely;

(3) it would similarly be against the public interest if the Commission met a very high rent, e.g. for a luxury flat in an expensive neighbourhood.

In recent years, the Commission has been able to rely increasingly on decisions made by rent tribunals, rent officers and rent assessment committees which have had the task of fixing reasonable or 'fair' rents. Once a rent had been fixed by one of these bodies, it was accepted for supplementary benefit purposes as being reasonable for the accommodation, though this did not necessarily mean that the accommodation would be regarded as reasonable for the claimant. The Housing Finance Act and the Housing (Financial Provisions) (Scotland) Act will lead to more rents being fixed in this way and will also involve local authorities not only in fixing 'fair' rents (standard rents in Scotland) for council housing but also in estimating the fair rents of private accommodation for the purpose of calculating rent allowances (if this has not already been done by the rent officer) and considering whether such accommodation is under-occupied or situated in an area of exceptionally high rents. These decisions are bound to have an important influence on the Commission's judgement as to whether a rent can be accepted as reasonable and, if not, how much of it should be included in the claimant's requirements. Precisely how the new arrangements will work, however, and in particular how much discretion will remain in the hands of the Commission's officers, it is too early to say. In broad terms, the situation is likely to be as follows:

(a) *Council housing*. Local authority rents will normally be accepted as reasonable, both for the accommodation provided and in relation to the circumstances of the particular claimant. Occasionally, however, where a council rent is so high that the rent rebate calculated according to the special rules explained on p. 39 has to be restricted so that it does not exceed the permitted maximum, the Commission may place a similar restriction on the amount of rent it is prepared to meet.

(b) *Private tenancies*. If the rent has been fixed by a rent officer or rent tribunal, the Commission will accept it as reasonable for the accommodation, but may decide that the accommodation is unreasonable for the claimant. If the tenant has applied for a rent allowance, and the local authority, in calculating the allowance, has decided that it should be reduced either because the dwelling is 'larger than he reasonably requires' or because the rent, owing to the location of the dwelling, is 'exceptionally high by comparison with the rent payable under comparable private tenancies of similar dwellings in the authority's area', the Commission will take this decision into account in deciding whether the accommodation is reasonable; but the Commission is not bound by the local authority's views on this point, and might possibly decide that the accommodation was not reasonable for the claimant even though the local authority had granted a rent allowance based on the full rent.

In cases where the rent has not been fixed by the rent officer or rent tribunal, and the tenant has not been awarded a rent allowance by the local authority, the Commission's officers have to use their own judgement in deciding whether the rent is reasonable, though they may well consult local council officials responsible for calculating the rent allowance to be awarded after eight weeks if the claimant is then still in receipt of benefit. If the tenancy does not fall within the scope of the rent allowance scheme, the levels of rent established locally by the rent officer, though not directly relevant, may still provide some guidance. In addition, it has been the practice in the past (and this will presumably continue) to lay down broad limits within which, in a particular area, rents will normally be met in full by the Commission. These limits are not published, but a typical figure for a house or flat in the south of England might be around £7 a week. If the rent and rates exceed the local limit for the type of accommodation, the decision as to how much should be allowed and for how long is taken by a senior officer in either the local or regional office. The local rent limits have no legal significance and are merely laid down for the guidance of officers and to ensure reasonable consistency of treatment, but there is a tendency for them to be applied rigidly, and the Commission has been known to refuse to meet a rent above the limit even where it was clear that the claimant could not expect to find cheaper accommodation. It should be noted that the appeal tribunal is not bound by the local rent limits and will probably not even know what they are. If the limits are applied unreasonably, therefore, it may be worth appealing to the tribunal.

The question of what is a reasonable rent to be met from public funds is complicated by the fact that after eight weeks the claimant will qualify for a rent rebate or allowance – or, if he is already receiving one, it will be recalculated at that point. The Commission will have regard to the full unrebated rent in deciding whether it is reasonable for supplementary benefit purposes. If it decides that the full rent is not reasonable, the tenant will be left to find part of it in other ways (normally out of the part of his weekly benefit intended for other purposes), whether he is actually paying the full rent or having part of it met by the local authority in the form of a rent rebate or allowance.

Example: A claimant living in private unfurnished accommodation pays a weekly rent of £10 and, on first claiming supplementary benefit, is not in receipt of a rent allowance. The Commission considers the rent unreasonably high and allows only £8 of it in assessing his requirements. If, before claiming supplementary benefit, he had already been awarded a rent allowance of £3, based on a fair rent of £8, the Commission would allow only £5. In either case, therefore, the amount of rent not covered either by supplementary benefit or by the rent allowance is the same – £2.

This means that when supplementary benefit has been in payment for eight weeks and the rent allowance is either awarded for the first time or revised, the claimant's disposable income, after paying the rent, will normally remain unaltered, the weekly benefit being adjusted to take account of the change in his net rent, still leaving the same amount (£2 in the above example) to be found from other sources.

Having decided that a particular rent is unreasonable (or that the accommodation is unreasonable for the claimant), the Commission may still feel that, in the circumstances of the particular case, it ought nevertheless to be met in full, at least for a time. One fact which may have to be taken into account is that certain groups in the population tend to be discriminated against by landlords and may therefore have great difficulty in finding accommodation at reasonable rents. They include coloured people, unmarried mothers, large families and other 'undesirable' tenants. Moreover, tenants in these vulnerable categories may be understandably reluctant to antagonize their landlords by applying to the rent officer or tribunal to get their rent reduced. To what extent should the Commission take these facts into account in deciding whether a rent is reasonable? There is no simple answer. All one can say is that the criteria applied in other cases should be applied with greater flexibility in cases of this kind.

If it is considered unreasonable to meet the whole of the rent on a long-term basis, the Commission may still be prepared to meet it temporarily, provided that:

(1) there are no other resources available to cover the rent commitment;

(2) the commitment cannot be immediately reduced; *and*

(3) the rent is not so high that it would be out of the question to meet it.

Once again, the policy quoted here from the *Handbook* is not always carried out; it is rare to find that a high rent is being met in full on a temporary basis, even where the three conditions are satisfied. Often, however, the first condition is not satisfied either because the claimant has resources such as an allowance from relatives which would normally be disregarded in calculating his weekly benefit (see pages 63–4) or because the high rent is connected with the presence in the household of a non-dependent member who can afford to pay more than his proportionate share of the rent.

Where the full rent is being met on a temporary basis, how long it is reasonable to expect this to continue will depend mainly on how much time is needed to reduce the rent commitment by moving, sub-letting, taking in boarders or getting the rent of the existing accommodation reduced. So long as active steps are being taken in at least one of these directions, the Commission should be prepared to continue meeting the rent in full. But the length of time for which benefit is likely to be needed is also an important consideration. It would be unreasonable to expect the claimant to move house or sub-let simply because he has to claim benefit during a short spell of unemployment or sickness, and in cases of this kind the rent should be met in full by the Commission for a few weeks at least, in all but the most exceptional cases.

The main point to remember is that whether a given rent is reasonable or not can only be decided in the light of all the circumstances of the particular case. In one case a rent of £3 may be unreasonable; in another, a rent of £12 may be reasonable – and it is by no means unknown for the Commission to meet a rent as high as this. It is a matter of judgement, and, if the Commission's judgement seems wrong, there is always a right of appeal.

House owners

If a claimant owns his house or is buying it by means of a mortgage, he is still entitled to have a weekly sum included in his requirements in respect of 'rent'. This will cover the rates, ground rent (if any), an allowance for repairs and insurance, and part of the mortgage payments. It will be adjusted as explained above if there are non-dependent members of the household or if part of the house is let to another family. The method of calculation is as follows:

(a) *Rates and ground rent.* Actual amount payable per week (e.g., for rates, divide the half-yearly amount by 26).

(b) *Repairs and insurance.* The Ministry of Social Security Act provides that 'a reasonable allowance towards any necessary expenditure on repairs or insurance' shall be included in the calculation of 'net rent'. The Commission allows a sum varying with the rateable value of the premises: see Table 3.

TABLE 3

Rateable value (assessed rental in Scotland)	Allowance
England and Wales:	
£55 or less	£10 a year
Over £55 up to £80	£10 + one fifth of excess over £55
Over £80	£15 + one eighth of excess over £80
Scotland:	
£40 or less	£10 a year
Over £40	One quarter of the rateable value

These amounts were fixed some years ago, and were probably inadequate even then. At present-day prices, they come nowhere near covering the average cost of repairs and insurance. The Commission takes the view that to make a weekly allowance for house repairs is unrealistic because the money is most unlikely to be put aside week by week to pay for major repairs, which only occur at infrequent intervals and are often unpredictable. It therefore prefers to deal with the problem when it arises by making a lump-sum 'exceptional needs payment'. (See pages 85–7.) At first sight, this may seem a reasonable policy, but it does not operate fairly in practice. While it is true that the Commission is often prepared to make lump-sum payments for repairs, it can only do so if it is aware of the need, and claimants do not always report such needs, either because they are reluctant to ask for extra grants or because they do not know help is available. Another objection to the practice of relying on lump-sum payments to meet the cost of repairs is that when the money is needed the householder may be back in full-time work and therefore no longer entitled to help from the Commission. A claimant who owns or is buying the house in which he lives should therefore ask for a realistic allowance to be made for repairs and insurance and, if this is refused, would have a strong case for an appeal to the local tribunal. Just what is a realistic allowance depends to some extent on the age and condition of the house but, generally speaking, a third of the rateable value (or a half in Scotland, where rateable values tend to be lower), with a minimum of £26 a year (50p a week), would not be excessive for a house in reasonably good condition.[1] If the house is in a bad state and the claimant is likely to be in receipt of benefit for a long time, a lump-sum payment should be requested at the outset to enable any necessary repairs to be carried out at once, in addition to the normal weekly allowance.

(c) *Mortgage payments.* Only the interest on the mortgage can be included in the rent allowance, not the capital repayments. The reason for this is that it is considered wrong that public money should be used to help a private individual acquire a permanent asset; though the same objection apparently does not apply where the help takes the form of an improvement grant, tax allowances on new industrial buildings, or the sale of council houses below market price. To find out how much of each mortgage payment is interest and how much is capital, it is usually necessary to ask the lender (building society, local council, etc.) to supply the figures. The claimant can do this himself or authorize the social security office to approach the lender on his behalf.

Once a decision has been made as to the amount to be allowed weekly in respect of mortgage interest, that amount remains unaltered so long as the mortgage payments continue at the same rate, even if there is a reduction in the amount of interest included in each payment. The reduction may be due to a fall in interest rates, or simply to the fact that, as the mortgage debt is reduced, the interest element in the payments falls and the capital element rises (this is usually the case, but not always, since there is a variety of methods of repaying a mortgage). It may therefore happen, particularly where benefit has remained in payment over a long period, that the amount

1. See P. A. Stone, *Urban Development in Britain: Standards, Costs and Resources, 1964–2004*, Vol. 1, *Population Trends and Housing* (Cambridge University Press, 1970), pages 141–6, for estimates of annual costs of maintaining housing. Note that Stone's figures are for 1964 and must be adjusted for price increases since then.

allowed for interest is considerably more than the actual interest currently payable and thus includes a contribution towards the capital repayments.

If benefit is payable only for a short period, however, the 'interest only' rule is applied rigorously. It often seems unfair, since the full amount of the mortgage payments, including both capital and interest, may be less than the rent payable for similar accommodation. The rule, however, is laid down in the Act, and the Commission has no discretion in the matter (the concession mentioned in the last paragraph is, strictly speaking, unlawful). In practice, hardship can usually be avoided by asking the lender to agree to only the interest being paid while the borrower is in receipt of supplementary benefit. Most lenders will agree to this but sometimes there are difficulties, particularly if the payments are already in arrears; and, of course, deferment of capital repayments means that it will take longer to pay off the mortgage. Moreover, some people may not want to make such a request, and there will anyway be little point in doing so if they are likely to be in receipt of benefit for a short time only.

There are two other possible ways of getting around the 'interest only' rule. One is to sub-let part of the house. The net proceeds of sub-letting (calculated as explained on pages 42–3) will be regarded as available to meet the capital repayments on the mortgage and, to the extent that they are needed for this purpose, will not be deducted in calculating the 'rent' allowance. For examply, if the capital repayments are £3 a week and the net proceeds of sub-letting are £4, only £1 will be deducted from the amount allowed for 'rent' (mortgage interest, rates, etc.). This concession is given by the Commission under its discretionary powers and only if it is satisfied that the claimant has no other means of meeting the capital repayments and has obtained whatever reduction the lender is prepared to allow.

The other possible solution is to obtain an allowance or lump-sum grant from a charity or some other source. Provided that the money is given for the express purpose of meeting the capital repayments, it will be ignored by the Commission. If it is not earmarked in this way, the Commission may not be willing to adopt this procedure, but it may still be worth appealing to the local tribunal, which is likely to take a sympathetic view of this type of case.

The 'unreasonable rent' rule applies to people who own their houses in the same way as to those who pay rent as such. Having calculated the net 'rent' as explained above, including mortgage interest, the Commission has to decide how much of it is 'reasonable in the circumstances'. The same local limits above which rents are not normally met in full are applied in considering whether the mortgage interest, rates, etc. are reasonable. While the use of these limits obviously simplifies the work of the Commission's officers, the results can be most unfair, especially where, for example, a deserted wife has to keep up the mortgage payments on her home. If a tenant is paying an unduly high rent, he can take steps to get it reduced; but once a house has been purchased, however exorbitant the price may have been, there is no way of reducing it. Besides, the size of the mortgage payments depends not only on whether the purchase price was fair, but still more on the prevailing level of house prices and interest rates at the time of purchase. It does not seem realistic, therefore, to limit the 'rent' allowance of an owner-occupier to a figure based on the current level of rents in the area.

In deciding whether the housing costs of an owner-occupier ought to be met in full, it should also be borne in mind that a move to less expensive accommodation, which may sometimes be possible for a tenant, is normally out of the question for a house owner, at least in the short run. Unless there is a possibility of letting part of the house or taking in a lodger, he is unlikely to be able to reduce his outgoings (apart from the capital repayments, which are anyway excluded from the rent allowance). The Commission should therefore be prepared to meet them in full in nearly all cases. Refusal to do so will normally constitute strong grounds for an appeal to the tribunal.

Rental purchase

This is a method of buying a house found mainly in Liverpool, Manchester and other places in the north-west of England, and generally confined to property of low value, often due for demolition within a few years. It has more in common with hire purchase than with the normal method of borrowing money on a mortgage for the purchase of a house, since ownership of the house does not change hands until the final instalment has been paid, though the purchaser is allowed to occupy it meanwhile. In some cases a legal contract is drawn up. In others there is merely a verbal agreement that, after paying so much per week for a given period, the tenant will become the owner of the house.

Where there is a written agreement from which it can be ascertained that a certain proportion of the total sum payable represents interest on the purchase price, the Commission calculates the amount to be allowed for 'rent' in the same way as if the house were being purchased by means of a mortgage, allowing the interest but not the capital element in each payment, plus the rates and an allowance for repairs and insurance based on the formula given on page 49. If no separate figure for interest is obtainable, the payments are treated as rent and allowed in full provided that they do not exceed the local rent limit. (See pages 45–6.) When this method is adopted, however, no allowance is made for repairs and insurance.

Since there is no mortgage, rental purchase arrangements are not, strictly speaking, covered by the 'interest only' rule. It would therefore be possible for the Commission to allow the weekly payments in full, regardless of how much of each payment is for interest and how much for capital. This, however, would have to be done on a discretionary basis unless it could be argued that the payments were really rent rather than instalments of the purchase price. Whether the Commission ought to allow anything for repairs and insurance depends on whether these are the responsibility of the claimant or not, but if such an allowance is made it should be adequate, taking into account the age and condition of the house.

Caravan dwellers

A claimant who is renting a caravan is entitled to a rent allowance calculated in the normal way. If he is buying the caravan on hire purchase or paying instalments under a credit sale agreement, the Commission can take the payments into account in assessing his weekly requirements, under its discretionary powers. Usually, however, as with rental purchase of a house, only the interest element in the weekly payments is allowed, although payments of this kind are clearly not covered by the provisions of the Act relating to mortgages. The argument that it would be wrong for the Commission to help a claimant to acquire a permanent asset does not apply here, since a caravan cannot be regarded as a permanent asset in the same sense as a house. Nor will it usually be possible to persuade the finance company to defer the capital payments. The claimant should therefore ask for the payments on the caravan to be taken into account in full in calculating his benefit and, if this is refused, he should consider appealing. In at least one recent case the Commission did agree to allow the full amount of the H.P. instalments on a caravan, and there is no reason why other cases should not be treated in the same way.

Rent in advance

Difficulties frequently arise where a claimant is moving into rented accommodation and has to pay a month's rent in advance. The Act defines 'net rent' for the purpose of calculating the rent allowance as:

(a) the rent payable for one week, and
(b) so much of any outgoings borne by the householder as is attributable to one week . . .

It is clear, therefore, that the benefit payable for any week can normally include only one week's rent. The Commission can, however, make an 'exceptional needs' payment to cover the balance of the first month's rent. (See pages 85–7.) In practice, this power is seldom used. The official view seems to be that the kind of accommodation that is suitable for a supplementary benefit claimant is normally let on a weekly rental basis and the payment of rent in advance therefore ought not to be necessary. This may be true in many parts of the country, but certainly not in all. In appropriate cases, the Commission should be pressed to use its discretionary powers for this purpose.

Overlapping rent

A very similar problem arises where a claimant is moving house and has to pay rent for a short period in respect of both his old home and his new one. Again, the only solution is an exceptional needs payment.

Payment of rent direct to the landlord

The Commission can pay benefit wholly or in part to somebody other than the claimant, if the claimant requests it or the Commission considers it necessary for the protection of his interests or those of his dependants (Ministry of Social Security Act, section 17(3)). This power is sometimes used to enable the Commission to pay the rent direct to the landlord. The Commission will normally only agree to this arrangement where benefit is likely to continue for a considerable period and the claimant is in arrears with the rent. To reduce the administrative work involved, the weekly rent is accumulated and paid over monthly to the landlord. If the landlord is the local authority, this causes no difficulty, but a private landlord may insist on the rent being paid weekly. In such cases, the Commission will sometimes pay the rent to a third party, e.g. a social worker, who passes it on weekly to the landlord.

As an alternative to paying the rent direct, the Commission sometimes pays only part of the benefit at the beginning of the week and holds the balance until evidence is produced that the rent has been paid. This can cause considerable inconvenience to the claimant, who must either call at the social security office weekly or send in the rent receipt by post and wait for the balance of the benefit to arrive. There is no right of appeal against the practice but, if it seems unreasonable in a particular case, the local office should be asked to revert to payment of benefit in the normal way at least for an experimental period, so that the claimant can demonstrate his ability to pay the rent regularly without compulsion.

There is a widespread belief, which the Commission appears to share, that a supplementary benefit claimant who gets behind with the rent is guilty of particularly serious misconduct, since he has misapplied public funds paid to him specifically for this purpose. This belief is based on a misunderstanding. It is true that the actual rent payable is taken into account in calculating the weekly benefit, but once the benefit has been paid the recipient is free to spend it as he wishes, just as he would be if it were a payment of wages. That is not to say, of course, that he is free to leave the rent unpaid, any more than a wage-earner would be. But getting behind with the rent is neither more nor less serious, from this point of view, than getting behind with the grocer's bill. Weekly benefit also includes money for groceries; the only difference is that the claimant is not told exactly how much. Getting into debt is always undesirable, but there is no reason why supplementary benefit claimants – who, after all, have more excuse for getting into debt than most people – should be made to bear a double load of guilt. Nor should their weekly benefit be reduced on the grounds that they are behind with the rent. If serious concern is felt about the possible consequences of allowing further rent arrears to accrue, the Commission should use its power to make future rent payments direct to the landlord.

Rate rebates

In any case where the Commission refuses to meet the rent in full on the grounds that it is unreasonable, the claimant should be advised by the social security office of his possible entitlement to claim a rate rebate and supplied with an application form to be forwarded to the local council offices. It is important that this should be done, since a person in receipt of supplementary benefit at the full rate cannot claim a rate rebate. (The same point arises in the case of claimants affected by the 'wage stop'; see pages 123–4.)

LIVING IN SOMEBODY ELSE'S HOUSEHOLD

So far, we have considered how a claimant's requirements are calculated if he or she is a householder, responsible for the rent or mortgage payments. Many claimants live in private households but are not themselves householders: for instance, a young person living as a lodger, or a pensioner living with a married son or daughter. They are treated either as 'non-householders' or as 'boarders'. It is important to distinguish clearly between the three categories – householder, non-householder, and boarder – because the category in which a claimant is placed can have a considerable effect on the amount of benefit he is entitled to, as a simple example will show:

Edward P. has a room in his aunt's house and shares the kitchen. He pays £2 a week rent for the room. He also pays his share of the electricity and other overheads. He buys and prepares his own food. As a *householder*, his requirements are assessed as £8·55. After some time, his aunt offers to provide him with meals and they agree on a board and lodging charge of £5. He thus becomes a *boarder* and, provided that this is accepted as a reasonable charge, his requirements will now be assessed as £7·10 – unless the Commission decides that he is not really a 'commercial' boarder but is staying with his aunt as one of the family, in which case his requirements as a *non-householder* will be assessed as £5·90 or, if he is under 18, £4·75.

Boarders

Instead of laying down a precise figure for the requirements of a boarder, schedule 2 of the Ministry of Social Security Act provides that they are to be assessed at 'such amount as may be appropriate', but not less than the normal scale rate. Provided that the Commission is satisfied that the board and lodging charge is reasonable, it normally takes the boarder's requirements as being this sum plus an allowance for clothes and other personal expenses. This allowance, fixed by the Commission and increased yearly in line with the scale rates, was raised to £2·10 for a single person in October 1972, and to £3·50 for a married couple. Thus, in the example above, Edward's requirements as a boarder are taken to be £5 plus £2·10, making a total of £7·10. If a boarder has children living with him, an additional allowance for clothing etc. is added (for a child under 5, 60p; aged 5–10, 75p; 11–12, 90p; 13–15, £1·15; 16–17, £1·35).

As usual, there are exceptions to the rule. There are two main reasons why a boarder's requirements may, in practice, be assessed at a lower figure: that the board and lodging charge is considered to be unreasonably high or that the arrangement is not a genuinely commercial one. The question 'What is a reasonable board and lodging charge?' is not very different from the question we have already considered, 'What is a reasonable rent?' The Commission will want to be satisfied that the charge is reasonable for the accommodation and services provided, which, particularly if the claimant is old or infirm, may go far beyond the basics of food, heating and cleaning. Comparisons will be made with the general level of board and lodging charges in the locality and, as in the case of 'unreasonable' rents, there will probably be a local maximum which officers will be reluctant to exceed. Allowance will, however, be made for any extra care given to an old or handicapped person which a boarder would not normally expect to receive.

The Commission will also want to be satisfied that the

standard of accommodation and services is reasonable in relation to the circumstances of the claimant. The official policy on this question is set out in the *Handbook*:

A supplementary pensioner is not normally expected to lower the standard of lodgings which he enjoyed when he was self-supporting, unless that standard is clearly higher than the accommodation in a modern Local Authority home or good class home run by a voluntary organization in the locality. Similarly, a claimant normally in the employment field will not be expected to lower the standard of his lodgings unless it is clearly higher than that of average commercial lodgings in the locality.

If the lodgings are considered unduly luxurious and it is suggested that the claimant should look for something more reasonable, he should anyway be put in a position to meet the charge in full on a temporary basis to give him time to move. As with high rents, it may be reasonable for the Commission to meet a board and lodging charge in full for a claimant who is likely to need benefit for only a short time, even if it is higher than they would be prepared to meet for a long-term claimant.

Bodies such as the Abbeyfield Society, which provide board and lodging for old people, sometimes come to an agreement with the Supplementary Benefits Commission as to the board and lodging charge that the Commission is prepared to meet in full. Provided that the charge does not exceed this figure, such an agreement will avoid the need for each case to be considered separately. It may happen, however, that the organization in question is obliged to make a higher charge, at least for some of its accommodation, in order to make ends meet. An old person paying this higher charge will be told that the Commission is unable to meet it in full because of the agreement. He has a perfect right to dispute this decision if he considers that both the accommodation and the charge are reasonable, since he was not a party to the agreement, which cannot therefore be considered binding on him.

Despite these occasional difficulties, the full board and lodging charge will usually be taken into account in assessing the claimant's requirements, provided that the relationship between the boarder and the landlord is a straightforward commercial one or the accommodation is provided by a voluntary body. A boarder living with close relations is treated differently and less generously. His requirements are assessed in the same way as those of a 'non-householder' (see below), this being the minimum permitted by schedule 2 of the Act. The Commission's unwillingness to take into account the actual board and lodging charge in such cases is understandable, since it would otherwise be very tempting for parents and children, for example, to agree on a weekly charge simply in order to obtain the higher rate of benefit for a boarder rather than the lower rate for a non-householder. But the results of this policy of treating close relations as 'non-householders' regardless of the financial arrangements between them often seem unfair. It is partly a matter of deciding what is a 'close' relationship. The example given by the Commission in the *Handbook* is 'parent and son or daughter', but in practice claimants living with brothers, sisters and, in some cases, more distant relations are also treated as 'non-householders', whether they are paying a fixed board and lodging charge or not, unless it is clear that the arrangement is a genuine commercial one which existed before the claim for benefit was made. Where the relationship between landlord and boarder is not that of parent and child, and a fixed weekly charge is in fact being paid, it is worth considering an appeal to the local tribunal if the Commission refuses to meet the board and lodging charge. The point to emphasize to the tribunal is that the case is covered by paragraph 17 of schedule 2 of the Act, which deals with persons paying an inclusive charge for board and lodging, and that under that paragraph such a person's requirements are to be taken as 'such amount as may be appropriate', the 'non-householder' rate being the *minimum*.

'Non-householders'

The requirements of a claimant living in somebody else's household and not paying an inclusive charge for board and lodging must be assessed at the rates shown in Appendix 1 for 'non-householders'. These rates vary with the age of the claimant, being lower for those under 18. A fixed allowance for rent (70p a week from October 1972) is added.

The non-householder rates are laid down in the regulations and must therefore be applied in the normal case. The Commission can, however, increase the amount of benefit payable if there are exceptional circumstances. (See page 72.) It uses this discretionary power in the case of a young mother living away from her parents, to whom it would obviously be unreasonable to pay a lower rate of benefit merely because she happens to be under 18. There are many other cases in which the Commission can reasonably be asked to exercise its discretion by paying more than the normal non-householder rate, though it will seldom agree to do so without an appeal. For instance, if the householder with whom a claimant is living has to pay a high rent, it can be argued that the rent allowance of 70p is unfairly low. Or again, it can be argued that any claimant under 18 who is forced to live away from home but does not qualify for treatment as a boarder should be paid at the full adult non-householder rate.

It should be noted that a claimant who is living in somebody else's house may be entitled to be treated as a householder, whether the owner or tenant of the house is a close relative of the claimant or a total stranger. It depends on the living arrangements. If he pays rent for the part of the house he occupies and prepares his own meals (even if he has only a bed-sitting room and shares the kitchen with the other occupants of the house), he can probably claim to be a separate householder entitled to the normal householder rate of benefit, including a rent allowance based on the actual rent he is paying. Similarly, if several people are sharing responsibility for the rent of a house and each is living as a separate household, though sharing cooking and other facilities, they should each be treated as a householder for benefit purposes. It will help in establishing that they are in fact separate households if the landlord can be persuaded to issue separate rent books to each of them. The fact that there is only a single rent book, however, does not necessarily mean that they are all living as one household. It is the actual living and financial arrangements that are the real test.

Chapter 3

HOW BENEFIT IS CALCULATED (2) RESOURCES

Chapter 2 was concerned with the claimant's 'requirements'. In later chapters we shall return to this subject in order to explain the treatment of a variety of special cases where the normal rules do not apply or allowance is made for extra needs. Meanwhile, we turn to the other side of the picture – the claimant's 'resources' which have to be set against his requirements in calculating the benefit payable.

The basic principle is that, if money is available from other sources to meet the needs of the claimant and his dependants, there is no need for the Commission to duplicate these resources. The Ministry of Social Security Act, however, provides (in part III of schedule 2) that a claimant may have limited amounts of income or savings (known as 'disregards') without any loss of benefit. The provisions are summarized in Table 4. Fuller details of some of the disregards are given below.

TABLE 4: RESOURCES TAKEN INTO ACCOUNT AND DISREGARDED

A. Resources taken into account in full

1. Family allowances
2. Family income supplement
3. National insurance benefits (except those mentioned under *B* and *C*)*
4. Industrial injury benefit
5. Payments, voluntary or under Court order, for the maintenance of a wife, ex-wife or children

* The national insurance attendance allowance for the severely disabled is taken into account in full, but a corresponding amount is included in the assessment of the claimant's requirements. See pages 36–7.

B. Resources wholly disregarded

1. Owner-occupied house
2. Furniture and personal possessions †
3. Business assets on which a person normally relies for his livelihood †
4. Maternity grant (the lump-sum national insurance benefit paid on the birth of a child, *not* the weekly maternity allowance which some mothers receive before and after the birth)
5. Death grant
6. Victoria Cross and George Cross annuities
7. Voluntary payments for purposes not covered by supplementary benefits (holidays, television rental, mortgage capital repayments, etc.) †
8. Occasional gifts in cash or kind †
9. Education maintenance allowance (higher school bursary in Scotland) †

C. Resources partially disregarded

The amounts disregarded are as follows:
1. £2 of net weekly earnings of:
    (a) claimant if not required to register for work
    (b) claimant's wife
2. £1 of net weekly earnings of:
    (a) claimant required to register for work
    (b) claimant's child under 16
3. £2 per week of the *total* of:
    (a) war and industrial disablement pensions
    (b) workmen's compensation
    (c) excess of war or industrial widow's pension over standard national insurance widow's pension
    (d) part of the children's allowance included in a widow's pension – 38p a week for first two children, 28p each for third and subsequent children
4. £1 per week of the *total* of
    (a) pensions and annuities, other than national insurance and war pensions
    (b) voluntary payments for purposes covered by supplementary benefits
    (c) profit from sub-letting
    (d) assumed income from capital of £325 or more (5p for each £25 between £300 and £800; 12½p for each £25 over £800)
    (e) any other income not mentioned above

(The total income disregarded under 3 and 4 must not exceed £2 per week.)

† Disregarded on a discretionary basis.

PART-TIME EARNINGS

The first £2 per week of the claimant's net earnings are ignored, unless he is required to register for work as a condition of receiving benefit (see pages 28–9), in which case only the first £1 is ignored. Similarly, the first £2 of the net earnings of the claimant's wife or of a child over 16 who is treated as a dependant are ignored, and the first £1 earned by a child under 16. In each case it is 'net' earnings that count, and this means what is left after paying tax and insurance contributions and 'any expenses reasonably incurred' in connection with the employment. Reasonable expenses would include fares to work and, in the case of a mother, the cost of having the children minded so that she can go to work. Trade union dues and pension contributions can also be deducted. The £2 of net earnings which are to be disregarded can thus be equivalent to £3 or £4 gross. If the amount earned in a particular week cannot readily be ascertained, the normal method of calculation does not apply. Instead, the week's earnings are to be 'calculated or estimated in such manner and on such basis as the Commission consider appropriate'. Part-time earnings from self-employment might, for example, have to be estimated. (The rules for computing net earnings are to be found in the Supplementary Benefit (General) Regulations 1966, Statutory Instruments, 1966, No. 1065.)

MISCELLANEOUS INCOME

(Section C, items 4 a-e, in Table 4.) Income qualifying for the £1 'disregard' may include such items as a private pension or annuity, regular payments from a charity or from friends or relatives, and income from capital, assessed as explained below. It can also include any 'profit' from sub-letting part of the claimant's home (if there is a mortgage; see page 51). But the total amount disregarded under headings 3 and 4 of section C in Table 4 must not exceed £2. For example, if the claimant has a disablement pension of which the first £2 is disregarded, the whole of any superannuation or assumed income from capital will be taken into account in calculating his benefit. If the disablement pension is only £1·50 per week, another 50p of weekly income under heading 4 can be disregarded.

DISCRETIONARY DISREGARDS

In addition to the resources which the Commission is *required* to disregard, wholly or partially, the Act provides that any other resources not specifically mentioned 'may be treated as reduced by such amount (if any) as may be reasonable in the circumstances of the case'. This discretionary power to disregard resources does not apply to national insurance benefits, industrial injury benefit, family allowances and maintenance payments by a man for his wife and/or children; these *are* specifically mentioned and must be taken into account in full. It does, however, enable the Commission to disregard occasional gifts, and payments intended to enable the claimant to meet expenditure which is not regarded as being covered by his weekly benefit. Examples given in the *Handbook* are 'payments for or provision of holidays, home decorating or major items of furnishings, the hire purchase or rental of a television or radio, mortgage capital repayments and part of a high board-and-lodging charge or rent not provided for in the assessment'. Education maintenance allowances (higher school bursaries in Scotland) for children staying on at school after the minimum school-leaving age are also disregarded on a discretionary basis.

TREATMENT OF SAVINGS AND OTHER CAPITAL RESOURCES

Many people still believe that it is necessary to be more or less destitute before one can claim supplementary benefit. This is far from the truth. A claimant who owns his house and has £1,000 or more in the bank may still qualify for benefit.

The value of an owner-occupied house is ignored completely. In practice the Commission also ignores personal possessions, including furniture (the days when a family was expected to sell the piano before seeking help from public funds are happily long past), and 'the capital value of a business on which a person (for example, someone who is temporarily sick) normally relies for his livelihood' (*Handbook*, paragraph 22). The aim is to take into account only those resources which can reasonably be regarded as available to meet the claimant's current expenses.

The value of all other savings and investments of all kinds is totalled and treated as being equivalent to a weekly income according to a 'tariff' laid down in the Act. If the total capital comes to less than £325, it is ignored altogether. For every complete £25 between £300 and £800, a weekly income of 5p is assumed, while each £25 above £800 is assumed to produce 12½p per week. The actual income produced by investing the capital is ignored. It may be more or less than the assumed income. If the capital amounts to much over £800, the actual income will probably be less, since the assumed income of 12½p per week on £25 is equivalent to an annual interest rate of 26 per cent. The assumption underlying this high rate is that, if the claimant has a substantial amount of capital, he can reasonably be expected to use some of it to meet his current living expenses.

Table 5 shows the assumed weekly income derived from different amounts of capital. As the assumed income from capital is included in the £1 of 'other income' which can be disregarded, it can be seen from the table that it is possible to have as much as £824 savings without any reduction in benefit. This would be the case, for instance, for a retirement pensioner with no income other than his pension and the interest on his savings. The precise amount of savings he could have while still qualifying for some benefit would depend on his circumstances and, in particular, on the amount of his rent.

In spite of these provisions for ignoring small savings and

TABLE 5

Amount of Capital			Assumed Income	Amount of Capital			Assumed Income
Less than		£325	Nil	£700 but under		£725	80p
£325 but under		£350	5p	£725	,,	£750	85p
£350	,,	,, £375	10p	£750	,,	£775	90p
£375	,,	,, £400	15p	£775	,,	£800	95p
£400	,,	,, £425	20p	£800	,,	£825	£1·00
£425	,,	,, £450	25p	£825	,,	£850	£1·12½
£450	,,	,, £475	30p	£850	,,	£875	£1·25
£475	,,	,, £500	35p	£875	,,	£900	£1·37½
£500	,,	,, £525	40p	£900	,,	£925	£1·50
£525	,,	,, £550	45p	£925	,,	£950	£1·62½
£550	,,	,, £575	50p	£950	,,	£975	£1·75
£575	,,	,, £600	55p	£975	,,	,, £1,000	£1·87½
£600	,,	,, £625	60p	Thereafter 12½p for			
£625	,,	,, £650	65p	each extra £25.			
£650	,	,, £675	70p				
£675	,,	,, £700	75p	e.g.		£2,000	£7·00

the income produced by them, it is still true that a person who has providently put money aside for a rainy day may find that, as a consequence of his thrift, he is treated less generously by the State than if he had simply spent all his income as he received it. He may therefore be tempted to get rid of his capital in some way, for instance by giving it to his children, so that he will no longer be penalized by the Supplementary Benefits Commission. The Act guards against any such action by providing that 'if a person has deprived himself of any resources for the purpose of securing benefit or increasing the amount thereof those resources may be taken into account as if they were still his'. He may, on the other hand, decide to invest his savings in a house, the value of which, provided that he lives in it himself, will be disregarded. By doing so he is not depriving himself of his resources but merely investing them.

DISREGARDING THE 'DISREGARDS'

Although, as explained above, certain resources are disregarded in calculating the basic weekly benefit to which the claimant is entitled, the existence of these resources can be taken into account in deciding whether an additional payment should be made, either on a weekly basis or as a single lump sum, to meet a special need. See pages 84–6.

THE DISTINCTION BETWEEN INCOME AND CAPITAL

It is sometimes difficult to decide whether resources should be regarded as income or as capital. Wealthy taxpayers are well aware of the advantages of capital over income, and the same is true for supplementary benefit claimants except that they have fewer opportunities of planning their affairs accordingly.

A simple example is that of PAYE tax refunds. If an unemployed man receives a tax refund, should it be treated as income for the week in which it is received or as capital? If it is income, all but the first £1 per week will be deducted in full from the man's supplementary allowance (unless the Commission uses its discretionary powers to ignore it). If it is capital, it will be disregarded unless the man's total capital resources, including the refund, amount to £325 or more, and at worst it will be 'taxed' at ½ per cent per week. In this instance, the Commission usually adopts the more generous interpretation, saying, in effect, 'A tax refund is money which was already yours and which the tax office is now returning to you'. (PAYE refunds to strikers and certain other claimants are treated as income under the Social Security Act, 1971; see pages 129–30.)

In other cases, however, the Commission's attitude is sometimes less generous. The most frequent type of case where doubt can arise is that of a claimant who has recently received a payment from his last employer. If the payment represents wages for the previous week, it is clearly income and must be taken into account in full, subject to the earnings disregard of £1 or £2. Similarly, if the employment was monthly paid, the previous month's salary must be regarded as income. But for what period should the claimant's needs be assumed to be covered by his last wage or salary payment? What if it includes, in addition to the normal payment, any of the following: holiday pay, a week's wages 'in hand', commission or bonus for the previous quarter, arrears due under a back-dated pay award, or a redundancy payment, official or otherwise? There is obviously a case for regarding all these additions as accumulated savings rather than as current income. The Commission's policy is to assume that a normal payment of wages or salary will meet the claimant's requirements until the time when, if he had remained at work, he could normally have expected a further wage or salary payment. If the payment is substantially higher than his requirements for that period by supplementary benefit standards, he may be expected to manage on it for up to a week longer. In most cases, however, a week's wages are assumed to last for a week, a month's salary for a month. Wages 'in hand' and holiday pay are treated in the same way, as income rather than capital: if the claimant has received, with his last week's wages, a week's holiday pay, he will be expected to manage for two weeks on this sum. But a single week's wages, even if it includes extras such as commission or bonus, will simply be treated as income available for that week, and similarly with any extras included with a month's salary. If the Commission's policy on this point seems unfair, the claimant should appeal. The tribunal may well decide, for instance, that he should be allowed to put his holiday pay aside for the purpose for which it was intended, and that it should not be regarded as income available to meet his immediate needs.

Redundancy payments, if they take the form of a lump sum, are treated as capital. This applies both to payments under the official redundancy payments scheme and to unofficial 'golden handshakes' paid by employers. If redundancy payments take the form of a weekly income (e.g. in the mine-workers' scheme), they are treated as income for supplementary benefit purposes, subject to the usual £1 disregard for miscellaneous income. See pages 65–6.

Disablement gratuities paid under the industrial injuries scheme, where the degree of disablement is assessed at less than 20 per cent, usually take the form of a lump sum and are treated as capital. Sometimes, however, the assessment is made for a limited period such as a year, and the lump sum will then be treated as income and spread over the number of weeks to which it relates – e.g. a gratuity of £52 in respect of an assessment made for one year would be treated as a weekly income of £1. This would normally be covered by the £2 disregard, but it could result in a reduction of supplementary benefit if the £2 disregard was absorbed by income from other sources.

Chapter 4

ABOVE THE MINIMUM

So far we have been concerned with the way in which a claimant's requirements and resources are calculated where there are no exceptional circumstances. By subtracting total resources (less 'disregards') from total requirements, we arrive at the minimum benefit payable, subject to certain exceptions explained in the next chapter. But the Supplementary Benefits Commission can and often does pay more than the minimum amount arrived at in this way. It can do so either by increasing the weekly rate of benefit or by making additional lump-sum payments for particular needs.

The power to make *discretionary additions* to the weekly benefit payments is conferred by paragraph 4(1)(a) of schedule 2 of the Ministry of Social Security Act, which says that where there are exceptional circumstances benefit may be awarded at a higher rate 'as may be appropriate to take account of those circumstances'. The power to make lump-sum *exceptional needs payments* is given by section 7 of the Act, which reads as follows:

Where it appears to the Commission reasonable in all the circumstances they may determine that benefit shall be paid to a person by way of a single payment to meet an exceptional need.

Before considering some of the ways in which these powers are or could be used, there are some general points which should be stressed.

The first point to note is that there is virtually no limit to the purposes for which discretionary additions and exceptional needs payments can be given, except that medical and similar requirements are in general excluded by section 6 of the Act. The only condition that must be satisfied is that there

72

is an 'exceptional circumstance' or an 'exceptional need' in the particular case. Thus the normal everyday needs of food, clothing, fuel and light are regarded as being covered by the basic scale rates unless, for example, additional heating is required because of age or sickness or a special diet has been prescribed by the doctor. Yet even normal needs of this kind can be the subject of an exceptional needs payment if an expensive item of clothing is needed or (more rarely) a debt has been incurred for, say, electricity and there is a danger of hardship as a result of supplies being cut off if it is not paid at once. In most cases, therefore, the important question is not whether the Commission has the power to meet an exceptional need, either on a weekly or a once-for-all basis, but whether it is prepared to use that power. And that brings us to the second point which must be emphasized: that both these types of payment are discretionary. We have already touched upon this point in Chapter 1, in considering to what extent supplementary benefit can be regarded as a right. For practical purposes it is best to assume that discretionary additions and exceptional needs payments are *not* a right, although the Commission's policies as set out in the *Handbook* or elsewhere can provide a powerful argument for the exercise of its discretionary powers in particular cases. In the last resort, if such arguments fail, the Commission is perfectly entitled to say 'No', though it should of course have reasonable grounds for doing so and there is always a right of appeal to the local tribunal. (We may note in passing that, while the tribunal is *obliged* to give reasons for its decisions, the Commission is not – but it can always be asked to do so.)

A final point to be noted is that, even if the Commission agrees that a special need exists, which is not covered by the basic scale rates, it does not necessarily follow that an additional payment of benefit will be made, since the claimant may be in receipt of a long-term addition (see pages 82–4), or may have other resources or access to other sources of help, on which the Commission feels he should rely for the purpose in question. The implications of this point will be explained in more detail below, but it is mentioned here because it is a frequent cause of misunderstanding and disappointment.

DISCRETIONARY ADDITIONS

The purpose of discretionary additions is to meet expenses of a regular nature which the claimant could not be expected to meet out of his weekly benefit calculated at the normal rate. Needless to say, if a claimant chooses to live at a higher standard than the supplementary benefit scale is intended to provide, the Commission is unlikely to award him a discretionary addition to cover the additional cost. Broadly speaking, additions are given for expenses which can either be regarded as essential or as clearly desirable on medical or other grounds.

Extra heating

The Commission seems to assume that the basic scale rates are sufficient to cover normal expenditure of about £1·20 a week on heating. This is an average figure covering the whole year. Any necessary expenditure above this level should be covered by a discretionary addition. It would not be practicable to make an exact calculation of the extra fuel consumption in each case, and the Commission therefore gives additions, payable all the year round, at one of three rates – at present 30p, 60p, and 90p – depending on the severity of the need. The circumstances in which allowances at each of these three rates are awarded to a claimant who is a householder are as follows:

The *30p rate* is given where

(a) The mobility of a householder claimant or dependant is seriously restricted by chronic ill health or through general frailty or old age; *or*

(b) The accommodation of a householder (without earning non-dependants aged 21 or over living with him) is either difficult to heat adequately or requires the use of an expensive form of heating.

74

The *60p rate* is given where

(a) A householder claimant or dependant is seriously ill and needs extra heating or is housebound; *or*

(*b*) Either the accommodation of a householder claimant is exceptionally difficult to heat, or it is difficult to heat and requires an expensive form of heating; *or*

(c) Both the conditions for the 30p rate are satisfied.

The *90p rate* is given where

(*a*) A householder claimant or dependant is bedfast and needs extra heating day and night, or is seriously ill and needs a constant room temperature day and night; *or*

(b) Conditions a and b for the 60p rate are both satisfied.

Similar additions are made where the claimant is not a householder but satisfies the health conditions set out above.

If the additional allowance given in a particular case is inadequate, a further increase can be requested. Such a request should be backed by evidence of the claimant's expenditure on fuel. A letter from the doctor confirming the need will also help.

A discretionary addition for heating may be given even if extra heating as such is not required, in cases where a fixed charge of more than £1·20 per week has to be paid for central heating. This occurs particularly in modern council flats. Since the charge is known and the individual tenant has no control over it, there should be no difficulty in obtaining a discretionary addition to cover the excess over £1·20 per week. Difficulties may, however, arise, where central heating has to be supplemented by other sources of heat. If the total cost of heating, averaged over the year, is more than £1·20 per week and it is clear that this is not due to unreasonable extravagance, a discretionary addition should be given.

Special diets

If a special diet is needed for medical reasons, a discretionary addition is given to meet the extra cost of food. A letter or diet sheet from the doctor or hospital is helpful as evidence of the need for a special diet. As in the case of heating allowances, the Commission does not work out the exact cost of the diet in each case but allows 40p per week for a special diet, except in the case of the following conditions for which a special diet addition of 92p is given:

(a) diabetes;
(b) peptic ulcer (including stomach or duodenal ulcer);
(c) conditions of the throat or larynx involving serious difficulty in swallowing;
(d) ulcerative colitis;
(e) 'active' or 'quiescent' respiratory (including pulmonary) tuberculosis.

These standard allowances are increased from time to time to take account of changes in food prices. They have been fixed by the Commission on the basis of medical advice, but it does not follow that they will necessarily be adequate to meet the needs of a particular case. If they are not, an additional allowance should be requested – but it must be remembered that the discretionary addition is not intended to cover the whole cost of the diet, but only the excess over the cost of a normal diet.

Domestic assistance

Discretionary additions are given to pay for domestic assistance to claimants who are unable to do cleaning and other domestic tasks unaided. It may be possible to obtain the services of a home help without charge through the social services department of the local authority, in which case the need for an additional allowance will not arise. Where a claimant has to pay for a home help or to make private arrangements, the Commission will normally meet the full cost by a discretionary addition, provided that the help is considered necessary and the charge reasonable.

Laundry

The first 10p a week spent on laundry is regarded as a normal expense for which an additional allowance is not required. A discretionary addition is given to cover the weekly laundry expenses in excess of 10p where (the *Handbook* explains), 'they are necessarily incurred because, through illness, incontinence, disability or infirmity, it is difficult or impossible for the recipient or his wife to do the washing, or where there are no washing or drying facilities in the home'. It should be noted that the Commission recognizes two quite separate grounds for giving help with laundry expenses: the illness or disability of the claimant on the one hand, and lack of facilities in the home on the other. In practice, discretionary additions are given more readily on the first of these grounds than on the second. There must be many claimants living in furnished rooms and similar accommodation who are forced to send their washing out or go to the laundrette but who do not receive an additional allowance to meet the extra cost.

Hire purchase

A discretionary addition can be given to enable a claimant to keep up the hire-purchase payments on articles of household equipment or furniture which are, in the words of the *Handbook*, 'absolutely essential'. There is of course room for argument as to what is absolutely essential but, generally speaking, the only items to which the Commission would be likely to apply this description are beds and bedding, a gas or electric cooker, basic floor coverings (lino, not carpets), and a table and chairs (but not armchairs or a sofa). Refrigerators, washing machines and other labour-saving equipment would not normally be regarded as essential, although it is possible that they might be in a particular case – e.g. a disabled person or a woman with a large family. A television set is definitely excluded!

Whether the Commission will in fact agree to meet hire-purchase payments by a discretionary addition depends on a number of factors. It is more likely to view such a request sympathetically if the hire-purchase commitment was undertaken at a time when the claimant could reasonably expect to be able to meet it out of his own resources; if the articles in question are not unduly expensive; and if a considerable proportion of the instalments has already been paid. If the claimant is likely to be on benefit for a long time, the Commission may well prefer to make an exceptional needs payment so that the balance of the purchase price of the articles can be paid off straight away, since this may be cheaper in the long run.

Telephones

A telephone is not normally regarded as an essential item of equipment for a supplementary benefit claimant, but there is one very limited type of case in which the Commission is prepared to give a discretionary addition to meet a telephone rental charge: 'a housebound person living alone who is dangerously isolated to the extent that a telephone in the house would be the *only* means of contact in an emergency' (*Handbook*, paragraph 65). These conditions are so stringent that the number of people who receive help with the cost of telephones from the Commission is extremely small. In the few cases where such help is given, it sometimes takes the form of an exceptional needs payment to cover the cost of installation rather than, or in addition to, a discretionary addition to cover the quarterly rental.

If a chronically sick or disabled person is in need of a telephone, whether on medical or social grounds, it is advisable to apply first to the local authority's social services department, which has a duty to provide help of this kind under the Chronically Sick and Disabled Persons Act, 1970. The circumstances in which such help can be given by the local authority are much broader than those in which the Commission is prepared to use its discretionary powers. A local authority, however, cannot help unless the person concerned is substantially and permanently handicapped. In other cases, if there are good reasons for arguing that the claimant needs to have a telephone, the Commission should be asked to help, even if the conditions laid down in the *Handbook* are not fulfilled.

National insurance contributions

As a general rule, the Commission does not give discretionary additions to enable a claimant to keep up his national insurance contributions. Such help, in fact, is not normally necessary. Pensioners do not have to pay insurance contributions. Persons in receipt of sickness or unemployment benefit can have their contributions 'credited', as can unemployed men who have exhausted their right to unemployment benefit. Married women who are not in employment do not have to pay contributions. Nor do most widows. And people classed as 'self-employed' or 'non-employed' whose income does not exceed £468 a year, excluding supplementary benefit, family allowances and certain other 'disregards', need not pay contributions provided that they obtain a certificate of exception. It would be very unusual, therefore, to find a person entitled to supplementary benefit on a regular weekly basis and still obliged to pay national insurance contributions. There are, however, two snags. The first is that few people bother to apply for a certificate of exception for short periods even though they may be theoretically entitled to do so. The second is that people who voluntarily choose not to pay contributions may find that their future right to national insurance benefits, including retirement pension, is affected. For example, a self-employed man who becomes unemployed and claims supplementary benefit does not have contributions credited to him and is therefore obliged to pay contributions at the 'non-employed' rate while he is out of work, unless he applies for a certificate of exception on grounds of low income. If he decides to pay up rather than spoil his contribution record, he will have to pay over £1 a week for a 'non-employed' stamp. But the Commission will not make a discretionary addition to his benefit to enable him to do so. The only exception is in the case of a woman who gives up paid work in order to care for sick or aged relatives and claims supplementary benefit. The Commission will make allowance for the cost of her insurance stamps to enable her to maintain her national insurance contribution record.

The fact that the Commission is prepared to make an exception in this one type of case serves to emphasize the unfairness of refusing to do so in other cases. It is therefore well worth considering an appeal to the tribunal. A point that should be stressed at the appeal hearing is that, if a supplementary benefit claimant is working part-time, his national insurance contributions are deducted in calculating his net weekly earnings and are thus, in effect, added to his supplementary benefit. (See page 65.) It is best not to await the outcome of the appeal, however, before applying for a certificate of exception, since the certificate will normally operate only from the date of application. An explanatory leaflet and application form NI 27 can be obtained from the local national insurance office.

School holidays

Families living on supplementary benefit for any length of time often find that the normal rates of benefit are far more difficult to manage on during the school holidays, when the children can no longer get free school meals. It is often suggested, therefore, that the weekly benefit should be increased during the holidays. The official answer to such suggestions has always been that the normal scale rates for children provide fully for the cost of feeding them and that free school meals are an extra bonus which the family receives during the school term. The Commission therefore refuses to give discretionary additions during the school holidays to pay for midday meals for the children. Whether this refusal is justified in principle is extremely doubtful. It seems reasonable to assume that, when the scale rates are given parliamentary approval, it is on the assumption that families in receipt of supplementary benefit will also claim the various 'fringe' benefits to which they are entitled – free school meals, free welfare milk, exemption from health service charges, etc. If this is so, it follows that the loss of what is by far the most valuable of these benefits during the school holidays must cause the family's standard of living to fall below what Parliament intended. The Commission can perhaps argue that a school holiday hardly constitutes an 'exceptional circumstance' and that it cannot give discretionary additions automatically to all families with schoolchildren during the holidays. It could, however, give such additions where the circumstances of the particular family were such that the loss of school dinners would cause hardship. At present, it seems, requests for help of this kind are automatically rejected, but an appeal against such a refusal might well succeed. Moreover, if discretionary additions were awarded by appeal tribunals in a number of cases, the government might be forced to reconsider the present policy on this point.

Other exceptional circumstances

It would be impossible to list all the purposes for which discretionary additions can be given, if only because it is the odd and unpredictable case that justifies the discretionary powers which Parliament has conferred on the Commission. The *Handbook* gives a few other examples:

(a) The cost of renting the safety gas cooker available for use by old, disabled, or infirm people;

(b) Continuing extra expense because of abnormally heavy wear and tear of clothing resulting from a disability;

(c) Furniture storage charges incurred for good reason;

(d) Fares to visit a relative in hospital. (See pages 163–6.)

But the fact that a particular type of case is not specifically mentioned in the *Handbook* does not mean that a discretionary addition cannot be given. Wherever a need exists which cannot reasonably be met out of the normal weekly benefit or other resources at the claimant's disposal, it is at least worth asking for an addition; and if the answer is 'We can't help', it is important to ascertain whether 'We can't' means 'We could if we wanted to but we won't', since the appeal tribunal may well take a different view of the ways in which discretion should be exercised.

THE LONG-TERM ADDITION

The circumstances in which the claimant's requirements are increased by the 'long-term addition' of 60p (85p if the claimant or his wife is over 80) were explained in Chapter 2. (See page 36.) Broadly speaking, the long-term addition is available to pensioners and to any other claimants who have been drawing supplementary benefit for two years or more for reasons other than unemployment. The object of this additional allowance, which was introduced by the Ministry of Social Security Act in 1966, was to give an automatic increase in benefit, without detailed inquiry into special needs, to those categories of claimants who, under the old national assistance scheme, had been most likely to receive discretionary additions. It was intended to replace many of the small discretionary additions which had previously been given for extra fuel, special diets and so on. Only where the claimant had extra needs which were not fully covered by the long-term addition would an additional discretionary allowance be necessary. When the long-term addition was increased by 10p in October 1972, however, it was decided that this amount should be ignored in considering the need for a special addition. The long-term addition, therefore, now comprises two elements:

(a) A 10p addition to the amounts allowed in the supplementary benefit scale for the basic needs of long-term recipients; and

(b) An extra 50p (75p for the over-80s) for needs which might otherwise be met by a discretionary addition.

The effect of (b) can be shown by two simple examples.

Example 1: A pensioner needs a special diet, estimated to cost an extra 40p per week, but has no other exceptional needs. Since the pre-1972 long-term addition of 50p is more than sufficient to cover the extra cost of the diet, there are no grounds on which a discretionary addition can be given.

Example 2: Another pensioner needs an extra 75p for heating and laundry. As this is more than 50p, a discretionary addition of 25p is given to cover the difference.

The long-term addition has led to a good deal of misunderstanding. The reason for this will become clear if we consider what will happen in each of the above examples when the pensioner reaches the age of 80. Pensioner 1 will receive an extra 25p per week, since the long-term addition will rise from 60p to 85p. Pensioner 2 will also get the higher long-term addition but will lose the 25p discretionary addition since the whole cost of his extra needs will now be covered by the long-term addition. Thus, although pensioner 2 admittedly has greater needs than pensioner 1, he will get no increase in benefit at age 80, while pensioner 1 will be 25p a week better off. It is all perfectly logical, but not very easy to explain to pensioner 2! Similarly, it is difficult to explain to a claimant whose special needs are covered by the long-term addition why benefit is payable to him at the same rate as if those needs did not exist. Whether the logic of the situation is accepted or not, however, the fact is that the Commission is obliged to take into account all but 10p of the long-term addition in deciding whether to give a further discretionary addition and, if so, how much. It was this apparent unfairness that led to the 10p increase in October 1972 being given on a different basis. Future increases in the long-term addition seem likely to follow the same pattern.

The long-term addition is not regarded as covering any special needs of a dependent child: only those of the claimant and his wife. For example, if extra laundry expenses are incurred because a child is enuretic, or if a child requires a special diet, a discretionary addition can be given, even if the extra cost could be met out of the long-term addition.

OTHER RESOURCES

If the claimant has resources (other than his house and savings under £325) which would normally be disregarded (see chapter 3), those resources may be taken into account in considering the need for a discretionary addition – but the Commission is not obliged to take them into account, and must therefore decide whether and to what extent it should do so in any particular case. What the Commission does in practice is to work out the total amount of disregarded income, including the assumed income from savings of £325 or more, but excluding gallantry awards, education maintenance allowances and payments for specific items not covered by the scheme (e.g. mortgage capital repayments), and to regard all but 50p per week of it as available to meet any special needs. For example, if the claimant has part-time earnings, of which £2 a week are disregarded in calculating his basic entitlement, £1·50 of the disregarded earnings will be taken into account in deciding whether a discretionary addition is required. If he is also entitled to the long-term addition of 60p, 50p of this will also be regarded as covering part of his special needs (as explained above), and a discretionary addition will be given only if those needs amount to more than £2 per week. The formula used by the Commission is therefore:

Special needs *less* all but 10p of the long-term addition (if any) *less* excess of disregarded income over 50p (if any) = Discretionary addition.

Since the practice of taking the whole of the disregarded income in excess of 50p into account for this purpose is discretionary, there is nothing to prevent the Commission from treating individual cases more generously, and there are often good reasons for doing so. For instance, it may seem undesirable to remove most of the incentive for a pensioner to do part-time work by reducing the amount of disregarded earnings from £2 to 50p – which would be the effect of the Commission's policy where the special needs of the pensioner amount to £2 a week or more. In such a case it might well be argued that the Commission ought not to regard any of the £2 disregarded earnings as available to meet the special needs. Similarly, if the disregarded income includes £1 a week from friends or relations or from a charity and, though not given for a specific purpose, is intended to pay for minor luxuries that the claimant would not otherwise enjoy, it would seem wrong that it should be used to pay for essential needs which could be met by a discretionary addition. It is a matter of judgement in each case how far, if at all, the Commission is justified in reducing or withholding a discretionary addition because of the existence of disregarded resources, but this is the kind of point on which an appeal tribunal will often adopt a more flexible approach than the Commission.

EXCEPTIONAL NEEDS PAYMENTS

The main difference between discretionary additions and exceptional needs payments is that the former are additions to the weekly benefit payments, intended to meet additional expenses of a recurrent nature such as extra heating or a special diet, while the latter are lump-sum payments to meet particular needs as and when they arise. Although section 7 of the Act empowers the Commission to make lump-sum payments only if the need is exceptional, many of these payments are for items which claimants would normally be expected to pay for out of their regular weekly benefit, such as replacements of clothing. The main purpose of exceptional needs payments, however, like discretionary additions, is to provide for needs which are regarded as not being covered by the basic scale rates.

As with discretionary additions, the Commission takes into account other available resources in considering the need for, and the amount of, an exceptional needs payment. The long-term addition is not taken into account for this purpose, but the Commission can and does take account of resources which are disregarded in calculating the weekly benefit. The first £100 of savings are ignored but savings above that level, if readily realizable (e.g. in a bank account and withdrawable at short notice), are regarded as available to meet any exceptional needs. For instance, if the savings amount to £120 and the amount required to meet the particular need is not more than £20, no payment will be made. If the amount required is more than £20 and the Commission decides to make a payment, it will meet the need in full, not just the excess over £20. Similarly, if there is disregarded income which, over a period of four weeks, would meet the need (ignoring the first 50p per week), an exceptional needs payment will not be made. But 'disregarded' income which is already regarded by the Commission as being used to cover extra weekly expenses (see pages 84–5) will not be taken into account in deciding whether an exceptional needs payment should be made. These rules, like those relating to discretionary additions, have been adopted by the Commission under its discretionary powers; the Ministry of Social Security Act (schedule 2, paragraph 6) merely says that 'regard may be had' to any resources that would otherwise be disregarded, and it is open to the Commission – or the appeal tribunal – to decide that a departure from the usual practice is justified in a particular case.

Apart from the claimant's own resources, there may be other sources from which help can be obtained: in particular, the local authority and voluntary bodies such as the Women's Royal Voluntary Service (WRVS). The Commission may take the view that these sources should be tapped before the possibility of an exceptional needs payment is considered. This point is discussed in more detail below, in relation to particular types of need.

Possibly the most difficult question which arises in connection with exceptional needs payments is how frequently they should be made. A family living on a low income for months or even years is likely to have many needs for which it would be reasonable to ask for a lump-sum grant. If all these needs were to be met in this way, the system would rapidly get out of control, with officers spending most of their time dealing with exceptional needs payments at enormous administrative cost. For this and, no doubt, other reasons, officers do not go out of their way to invite such requests. Once a claimant becomes aware that lump-sum grants are available to meet special needs, however, he is likely to request them from time to time. The result, inevitably, is that a minority of claimants account for far more than their proportionate share of requests for exceptional needs payments. By doing so, they are apt to gain a reputation as 'scroungers', though in fact they are only asking the Commission to make full use of the powers conferred on it by Parliament. The Commission therefore tries to ration its favours. 'Payments for exceptional needs', the *Handbook* warns, 'are not made at frequent intervals to the same claimant, except where an alternative method of handling the situation is not immediately practicable.' It is advisable to avoid making frequent requests for extra grants if possible, not only because the Commission's reaction to such requests will become increasingly negative, but because the appeal tribunal is also likely to be influenced by the fact that a number of exceptional needs payments have been made in the recent past. One way of reducing the frequency of grants is to ensure that when a request is made it is as comprehensive as possible. If both clothing and bedding are needed, for instance, it is better to ask for a grant for both at once than to ask for two grants at short intervals. Having said this, however, one must stress that, if an exceptional need exists, there is seldom anything to be lost by asking the Commission to meet it. There are probably far more cases where a need is not met because it is not brought to the Commission's attention than where a grant is requested and refused.

The *Handbook* gives a number of examples of the purposes for which exceptional needs payments are made. Each of these examples is discussed below.

Clothing and footwear

Clothing grants are the most common type of exceptional needs payment. The Commission is generally prepared to help with the cost of replacing major items of clothing, particularly if the claimant has been living on a low income for some time. Grants for minor items are made only as part of a larger grant: the *Handbook* states that 'a lump-sum payment is not normally made for clothing or bedding where the cost involved is less than £1'.

It is not always easy to decide what is a 'need' for clothing. For instance, how many pairs of shoes does a man need? Does a person who has an overcoat need a raincoat too? How many dresses does a woman need? As a guide to its officers in answering questions of this kind, the Commission provides them with a form (B/O. 40) to be completed in cases where a grant for clothing is being considered, which indicates the number of each type of garment that the Commission regards as constituting an adequate stock of clothing for an individual or family. This inventory, which has remained unaltered for many years, is reproduced in Appendix 3. It should not be assumed that, if a clothing grant is requested, the family's clothing stocks will automatically be brought up to the level indicated in the inventory. The Commission may take the view – especially if the claimant is likely to be back in work fairly soon – that he should be prepared to manage temporarily at a lower standard. It does, however, provide, as the Under-Secretary of State for Health and Social Security, Paul Dean, put it, 'a general standard against which claimants' requirements for clothing and bedding can be judged' (*Hansard*, 31 March 1971, col. *400*), and there is no reason why it should not be implemented in the majority of cases. It can hardly be said to be unduly generous.

A request for an exceptional needs payment for clothing (or for most other purposes) is invariably followed by a visit to the claimant's home by a social security officer to investigate the needs. The officer then reports back to the local office, where a decision is made as to the amount of the grant (if any). The home visit is the claimant's main opportunity of stating precisely what his needs are, and it is a good idea to make a list of the items needed, using the inventory in Appendix 3 as a basis, and hand a copy of it to the visiting officer. Preferably the list should state not only what is needed but also roughly how much each item is expected to cost at a reputable local store, assuming that goods of reasonable quality are bought. Local social security offices maintain their own lists of prices at which various articles of clothing and bedding can be purchased locally, and clothing grants are normally based on these prices. The result, all too often, is that the clothing actually bought costs more than the sum allowed, so that the claimant has either to supplement the grant from his weekly benefit or to manage without some of the needed articles. The discrepancy in prices is sometimes due to the claimant's being less familiar than the local office with the cheapest sources of supply, but more often it is a question of quality. The claimant wants to buy clothes that will last, and the prices on which grants are based, though generally not unrealistic, do not always allow good-quality clothing to be bought. If the claimant has priced the items himself when requesting the grant, he is in a better position to question its adequacy later should this prove necessary.

Some years ago, it was a common practice for the National Assistance Board to refer people in need of clothing to the WRVS (in those days it was just plain WVS), which kept stocks of clothes, mostly second-hand, for needy families. In theory this is no longer done unless there are good reasons why an exceptional needs payment would not be appropriate (e.g. if such a payment has already been made but spent on other non-essential goods). Nevertheless, claimants are still sometimes referred to the WRVS instead of being given a cash grant, even where there is no good reason for doing this. It is of course possible that the clothes obtained in this way may sometimes be of better quality than could have been purchased with a cash grant. It is, however, a vitally important principle that supplementary benefit claimants should have the same right as other citizens to buy their clothes in the shops, and should not be expected to accept second-hand – or even new – clothes from the WRVS or any equally worthy organization. If claimants choose to buy at jumble sales or second-hand shops, or even to apply to the WRVS, they have a right to do so; the essential point is that they should be free to choose. Once the need for clothing is acknowledged, therefore, an exceptional needs payment should always be made unless there are genuine grounds for refusing it, which will seldom be the case.

A more difficult question is that of deciding where the division of responsibility should lie between the Supplementary Benefits Commission and the local education authority, where the provision of clothing for schoolchildren is concerned. Education authorities can give help of this kind in two ways. One is by making grants towards the cost of school uniform. Most authorities have a school uniform grant scheme, under which parents whose incomes are below a certain level can claim a grant of a fixed amount, with smaller grants for those with slightly higher incomes. The details of these schemes, including the size of the grants and the qualifying levels of income, are left to each local authority to decide, with the result that wide variations are found between one area and another, and a few authorities do not give school uniform grants at all. Where schemes exist, they are usually confined to secondary-school children, although uniforms are required in some primary schools; and most authorities insist on an interval of two years between grants for the same child, while some refuse to give a grant during the child's last year at school.

Local education authorities also have a more general power (under section 5 of the Education (Miscellaneous Provisions) Act, 1948) to provide clothing (sometimes referred to as 'necessitous clothing') for a school child who appears 'unable by reason of the inadequacy or unsuitability of his clothing to take full advantage of the education provided at the school.'

Again, there are wide variations between different authorities in the way in which this power is used. Some have fixed income limits, as for school uniform grants, while others consider each case 'on its merits'; and some authorities do not give help of this kind at all. Where such help is given, it is available to primary as well as secondary-school children. If section 5 of the 1948 Act, quoted above, is interpreted narrowly, however, as it usually is, it limits the provision of clothing to cases of the most extreme need.

The Supplementary Benefits Commission, the *Handbook* states, 'does not, in any circumstances, pay for distinctive school uniforms for which Local Authorities have power to make grants'. The Commission's attitude on this question is entirely understandable. Since local authorities are specifically empowered to make grants for this purpose, it does not seem reasonable to expect the Commission to make good the deficiencies of those local authorities which fail to make use of this power. But what are parents to do if they happen to live in an area in which school uniform grants are not given? One possible answer is to seek help on grounds of general clothing need rather than specifically for school uniform: either 'necessitous clothing' from the education department or an exceptional needs payment from the Commission. Provided that the grant is for the appropriate types of garment – e.g. jacket and trousers – it can be used to obtain garments of the material and colour required by the school, though the parents may have to put something towards the cost. A second possibility, if the Commission refuses a grant, is to appeal to the local tribunal. The appeal is not likely to succeed, since the tribunal will probably endorse the Commission's attitude. It may, however, be an effective way of putting pressure on the local authority, especially if an official from the education department is invited by the claimant to attend the hearing as a witness and explain the department's policy to the tribunal. A third possibility is to ignore school uniform requirements altogether, since there is no legal obligation on parents to dress their children in uniform – but most parents will be reluctant to cause the child embarrassment by doing this.

If a family receiving supplementary benefit for more than a few weeks is in need of help with schoolchildren's clothing other than school uniform, the Commission will generally accept responsibility for giving such help, rather than leaving it to the education authority. But in spite of this, a considerable proportion of families given 'necessitous clothing' by education authorities are also receiving supplementary benefit, and some at least are referred to the education department by the Commission, possibly because exceptional needs payments for clothing have been made repeatedly in the past and the Commission is not prepared to make further grants of this kind. Provided that the family obtains the help that is needed and is not asked to accept either second-hand clothing or the supervision of a social worker in buying new clothes (an indignity imposed by some local authorities on recipients of 'necessitous clothing'), it may not matter much whether it is the Commission or the education department that helps. Occasionally, however, one hears of families being shunted back and forth between the education and social security offices, each of which seeks to lay the responsibility on the other.

The right answer to this dilemma of divided responsibility seems to be that, where specific provision is made by a local authority for meeting a particular need, as in the case of school uniform grants, it is reasonable to expect claimants to make use of such provision before asking for extra grants from the Commission; but where the local authority has only a general power to help those in need, as with 'necessitous clothing', the primary responsibility for meeting the needs of supplementary benefit claimants rests on the Commission. Where difficulties arise over the provision of clothing other than school uniform, therefore, there is usually every justification for taking the matter to the appeal tribunal if necessary.

Another questionable practice mentioned in the *Handbook* in connection with grants for clothing and footwear is that 'where the claims for exceptional help occur repeatedly in the case of people receiving a supplementary allowance, the Commission will consider making a deduction from the weekly allowance for a period to offset any lump-sum payment which has to be made.' In other words, the Commission makes a grant for clothing and then recovers it by instalments. This is probably illegal, since the Commission has no power to pay benefit on the basis that it is recoverable, except where benefit is paid on grounds of urgent need to a person in full-time work or after a strike. (See pp. 130–32 and 182.) The Commission would no doubt claim that the subsequent deductions are a legitimate use of its power to reduce benefit where there are exceptional circumstances, but it is unlikely that this interpretation would be upheld in the courts. The difficulty in cases of this kind where the Commission appears to exceed its legal powers is that, if its actions were challenged on these grounds, the result might be that claimants who now receive grants in the form of a loan would no longer receive them at all, since exceptional needs payments are anyway discretionary. It may therefore be advisable to turn a blind eye to the legal niceties of the situation and to concentrate on ensuring that the practice of recovering lump-sum grants out of subsequent weekly benefit payments is subjected to the most careful scrutiny in individual cases. If there is the slightest doubt whether the deductions are justified in a particular case (and there is likely to be considerable doubt in most cases), an appeal should be lodged. Certainly the mere fact that 'claims for exceptional help occur repeatedly' does not justify the recovery of grants.

Bedding, furniture and household equipment

The Commission recognizes that people living on supplementary benefit or similarly low incomes for long periods of time cannot be expected to pay for replacements of bedding and furniture out of their weekly benefit. Similarly, if a family on supplementary benefit moves into unfurnished accommodation for the first time, it is accepted that they will need help in acquiring essential furniture and household equipment. As with clothing, however, it is one thing to accept that the need exists and another thing to decide who should meet it and how.

Where sheets, blankets and pillows are needed, there should be no difficulty in obtaining an exceptional needs payment to raise the family's stocks to the levels indicated in the inventory in Appendix 3. Claimants should not be expected to accept second-hand goods from the WRVS or other welfare organizations. The same applies to articles such as cutlery, crockery and kitchen utensils.

Furniture is more problematic, and the Commission's stated policy on this matter has recently been reformulated. The first edition of the *Handbook*, published in May 1970, stated: 'Exceptional needs payments are made for major items of bedding and household equipment where these are necessary because existing items cannot be repaired, or because items such as beds, mattresses, tables, chairs, floor coverings, or gas cookers are required for the first time e.g. on rehousing by a Local Authority from furnished accommodation.' Any doubt as to the extent to which the Commission was prepared to make cash grants for such items, rather than refer claimants to the WRVS and other bodies for provision in kind, was dispelled by the following general explanation of the Commission's policy with regard to exceptional needs:

In some cases, the claimant's exceptional needs are of a kind which charitable bodies sometimes meet or help to meet. Where the need is one which ought to be met by the Commission, they do so, and the question of a reference to a charitable body does not arise. Where it seems that the need is one which in principle the Supplementary Benefits scheme is not designed to meet, then, and only then, the claimant is advised where appropriate, that a voluntary body may be willing and able to do so.

This, of course, did not mean that cash grants would necessarily be given to cover the cost of *new* furniture. Most people would regard good-quality second-hand furniture as perfectly acceptable, provided that it is furniture that they have chosen themselves. It is the right to choose that is essential, and this right appeared to be fully recognized by the Commission in May 1970.

By April 1971, when a revised edition of the *Handbook* was published, this section had undergone a sad transformation as a result of a case in which the Commission was criticized for dealing with the case of a family moving into a new council house in a way that seemed totally at variance with the policy set out in the *Handbook*. In the revised edition, the passage quoted above reads as follows:

Where the need is one which ought to be met by the Commission, it does so, usually by a lump-sum payment, but sometimes, where the need is for things like furniture, by making arrangements for it to be supplied from a furniture store of a Local Authority Department or a voluntary welfare organisation which is willing to help. These bodies can also sometimes help to meet needs which the Supplementary Benefits Scheme is not designed to deal with, and in such cases the claimant is advised where appropriate that a voluntary body may be able to assist him.

The Commission, in short, is not prepared to make exceptional needs payments for furniture – not even for second-hand furniture – if it can be obtained free from the local authority or a welfare organization. What this means in practice is usually that the claimant has to accept whatever unwanted furniture happens to be available in the local store. It may, with luck, be both clean and of good quality. Often it is neither. In some cases, claimants are invited to the furniture store to choose from the available stocks. In others, the first time the recipient sees his 'new' furniture is when it is delivered at his house – and it will be a brave man who refuses to accept delivery, however hideous the things may be. Similarly, although it should be noted that the Commission's officers are instructed to make sure that the claimant is satisfied with the furniture he has received (and presumably to offer him a cash grant if he is not!), few claimants are likely to express openly any dissatisfaction they may feel.

One can only hope that the Commission's policy regarding the provision of second-hand furniture will be reconsidered in the near future. Meanwhile, claimants must decide for themselves whether they are prepared to challenge the policy by appealing against the refusal of exceptional needs payments for furniture, by insisting on the right to choose, and by rejecting the furniture offered to them if they do not consider it suitable. Social workers can help by refusing to supply furniture from their stores in cases where the proper way of meeting the need is by a cash grant.

In many cases, the furniture required is not available from local authority or other sources and the Commission is prepared to give an exceptional needs payment. The question then arises what items of furniture should be included in the grant. In principle, the Commission will only pay for furniture that is regarded as essential, and the definition of 'essential' for this purpose is broadly the same as that adopted in relation to discretionary additions for hire purchase of furniture. (See page 77.) The items of furniture for which the Commission is normally prepared to make a grant are thus severely limited and do not include many items which most people would take for granted as an essential part of their homes; carpets and armchairs, in particular, are generally excluded. How far the Commission should be expected to go towards furnishing a claimant's home must obviously depend on the circumstances. If his financial situation is likely to improve in the near future, it may suffice to provide the bare essentials – lino, curtains, beds, table, chairs and cooker. If the family is living more or less permanently on a low income, the Commission should be prepared to go further and cover the cost of normal furnishings such as a carpet for the living room and easy chairs for the adult members of the household. If it refuses to do so and the refusal seems unreasonable, an appeal should be considered.

Sometimes the precise amount of a grant for furniture and household equipment is less important than its timing. If a family is moving into unfurnished accommodation, the basic furnishings must be acquired before the move, especially if there are children. This is accepted by the Commission, and the official policy is to investigate the needs and take whatever action is necessary in good time, so that the family does not have to move into an empty house. To make this possible, it is obviously necessary that the claimant should apply for an exceptional needs payment as early as possible and anyway at least a week before the move. Even when adequate notice has been given, however, delays often occur. The social security office sometimes insists on an officer visiting the new home to ascertain precisely what the needs are before a grant is even considered. This is clearly unreasonable. It may be necessary for a visit to be made before a final decision can be taken about, for example, the amount of additional storage space required, but there is no reason why an interim grant should not be made, covering the items that are known to be needed. Even if a physical inspection of the premises is considered necessary, it will usually be possible to arrange for this to be carried out before the family moves in.

Removal expenses

The Commission will usually agree to meet the cost of removal, provided that the claimant has good reason for moving house; but if he is being rehoused by the local authority following a demolition or clearance order or a compulsory exchange of tenancies, the local authority has power to pay for the removal and the Commission will expect it to use this power (if it refuses, the Commission should of course be asked to help). Differences of opinion occasionally occur as to whether a claimant has good reason for moving. Generally speaking, people do not move house unless there are fairly cogent reasons for doing so, but the Commission may refuse to pay on the grounds that the move was a matter of convenience or preference rather than of necessity. This is a question that can only be decided in the light of individual circumstances.

If the Commission agrees to pay for the move, it will expect the claimant to obtain quotations from several removal firms and to accept the cheapest. It is always advisable to check that the price is regarded as reasonable by the social security office before making final arrangements, though a grant should never be refused solely on the grounds that the expenditure was not approved in advance.

Redecorations

If a claimant is responsible for internal decoration of his home, the Commission can be asked to make a grant for 'essential redecoration', though any other person with whom the accommodation is shared may be expected to contribute to the cost. The grant will normally cover the cost of materials, provided these are not unduly expensive. On the question of paying for labour, the 1970 and 1971 editions of the *Handbook* reveal a change of policy, or at least of emphasis, not unlike that noted above in connection with furniture grants. In May 1970, the relevant passage read as follows: 'Where the labour is provided by a voluntary or other body a payment may be made for the cost of materials.' By April 1971, this had changed to: 'The Commission would expect to assist only with the cost of materials where the labour *could* be provided free of charge by a voluntary or other body' (my italics). In other words, if voluntary labour, usually unskilled, is available, the claimant is expected to accept it rather than ask the Commission to pay for a professional decorator to do the job. There has been a vast expansion of voluntary work of this kind, mainly for old people, in recent years. For an isolated or housebound pensioner, having his home decorated by a team of enthusiastic young people may be an exhilarating experience, and it can often lead to a valuable ongoing contact. Many claimants, however, would regard it as an unwanted and degrading invasion of their privacy. Moreover, the quality of work of this kind done by volunteers is extremely variable. It is, to say the least, questionable whether claimants unable to do their own decorating should be virtually forced to have it done by unskilled amateurs, but this appears to be the effect of the Commission's present policy. It is to be hoped that the Commission will reconsider its policy in the near future.

Seeking or starting work

The *Handbook* lists, among the purposes for which exceptional needs payments are made, fares to help a person to find work and the cost of such things as clothing and tools needed to start work. A presentable suit of clothes may be particularly important for a person seeking white-collar employment.

If a person who is unemployed or threatened with redundancy is considering the possibility of finding work beyond daily travelling distance from home, it is worth inquiring at the employment exchange about the employment transfer scheme, under which help of various kinds is available, particularly for people with dependants, who may qualify for a lodging allowance, assisted fares for visits home, removal expenses, help with fees for the sale and/or purchase of a house, a lump-sum rehousing grant and other forms of assistance. The scheme also provides fares for interviews in certain circumstances and for the initial move, for single people as well as those with dependants.

If help is not available under the employment transfer scheme, the Commission may be prepared to assist with the cost of fares for job interviews or to enable an unemployed claimant to move to an area where jobs are more plentiful or return to his home town, especially if he is in an area of high unemployment and has been out of work for a long time. Claimants are normally expected to pay for local journeys in search of work out of their weekly allowance, but if the cost of such journeys becomes substantial there is no reason why help should not be given.

The Commission's power to assist with removal expenses has already been mentioned, and it can be used to help a person moving to a job in another part of the country if such help is not available under the employment transfer scheme. It should be remembered, however, that once a person has been in full-time work for more than fifteen days the Commission's powers are limited to giving help in cases of urgent need.

If a married man moves away from home to look for work, the Commission will, if necessary, pay benefit to his wife to meet her needs and those of the children during his absence, leaving him to claim in respect of his own requirements at the local office in the area where he is living. If he is drawing national insurance benefits which include allowances for his dependants, he will of course be expected to send these allowances home each week. It is always advisable to discuss these arrangements with the social security office well in advance so that the necessary adjustments can be made.

Other travelling expenses

In other cases where an expensive journey by the claimant or his wife or children is necessary, the Commission should be asked to make an exceptional needs payment unless the journey is of a kind that some other body (e.g. the local education authority) can pay for, or allowance has already been made for the cost of the journey in the weekly benefit payment. Some of the more common kinds of journey and sources of help are as follows:

(a) *Hospital treatment.* Hospital patients receiving supplementary benefit or family income supplement can have their fares to and from the hospital paid by applying at the hospital and producing their order-book. Fares should be claimed at the time of the visit, but can be claimed later if necessary. Payment is normally made by the hospital. Patients not receiving supplementary benefit or family income supplement may also be entitled to help with fares if, by supplementary benefit standards, they cannot afford to meet the cost themselves. They should obtain a form from the hospital giving dates of the visit or visits and take or send it to the social security office. These arrangements apply both to in-patients and out-patients. If the patient cannot travel alone, the travelling expenses of an escort will also be paid. There are special arrangements for war disablement pensioners undergoing hospital treatment for their war disablement, whose expenses are paid by the Department of Health and Social Security without any inquiry into their financial situation.

(b) *Visits to relatives in hospital.* The normal arrangements regarding help with the cost of visiting relatives in hospital are described in Chapter 7 (see pages 163–6). Help with fares may also be given on grounds of urgent need to a person not receiving supplementary benefit but who cannot afford the fares, for example, to visit a close relative who is seriously ill.

Close relatives of patients in the 'special' hospitals – Rampton, Broadmoor, Moss Side and the State hospital at Carstairs – can claim travelling expenses for monthly visits in the same way. For those who do not qualify for help from the Commission, other arrangements are made under section 66 of the Health Services and Public Health Act, 1968, by which a quarter of the return fare is refunded by the hospital authorities.

There are also special arrangements for payment of travelling expenses for hospital visits by the wife of a war disablement pensioner, or by another relative nominated by him.

(c) *Visits to relatives in prison.* Help with the cost of visits by the wife or other close relative of a person serving a prison sentence of more than three months is provided by the Home Office. If the relative is in receipt of supplementary benefit, or has an income not much above supplementary benefit level and is not working full-time, the social security office will deal with the question of fares and the claim should be made there. Those in full-time work and with incomes around or below supplementary benefit level should apply to a probation officer. Visits are normally allowed every four weeks but extra visits will be paid for on the recommendation of the prison welfare officer, or if the prisoner's solicitor confirms that a visit is necessary for the purpose of discussing arrangements for an appeal. In addition to the fares, the cost of overnight accommodation is paid if this is necessary. The travelling expenses of children accompanying the visitor can also be claimed provided that the prison welfare officer considers it reasonable that they should do so.

(d) *Visits to handicapped children in hospital schools and special schools.* The local education authority may pay the whole or part of the expenses incurred by parents in visiting a handicapped child receiving special educational treatment away from home. Such help is given at the discretion of the local authority, but the Department of Education and Science has advised local authorities that regular visits are desirable, especially if the children do not normally return home for holidays, and that they can help with the cost if they are satisfied both that without a visit the child's educational treatment would be impaired and that the parents cannot afford it.

(e) *Visits to children in the care of a local authority.* The social services department of a local authority in England or Wales can, where necessary, assist parents with the cost of visiting children in care, if (as is usually the case) such visits are likely to help towards the aim of restoring the child to its family. Similar help can be given by social work departments in Scotland, which have considerably wider powers to give financial assistance under the Social Work (Scotland) Act, 1968.

(f) *Children sent to the care of relatives.* When a parent is already receiving supplementary benefit, or there is urgent need, the Commission will consider helping with fares to enable a child to be looked after by relatives, e.g. while the mother is ill or unavoidably absent. The local authority social services department (social work department in Scotland) can also help in such circumstances, and this may be a simpler solution if the parent is not receiving supplementary benefit.

(g) *Visits to local offices.* Section 17 (4) of the Ministry of

Social Security Act provides that the Commission 'may, if they think fit, defray travelling expenses incurred in connection with claims to benefit'. This power is used sparingly. Fares to the local social security office are only reimbursed if it is accepted that there was good reason for the visit and that the person could not reasonably have been expected to make the journey on foot. As payments under this provision, unlike the other types of payment for travelling expenses described above, do not count as 'benefit' payments, there is no right of appeal against a refusal.

Fuel debts and rent arrears

The Commission does not normally regard the payment of debts as falling within its responsibilities. If the debt accrued before the payment of supplementary benefit commenced, the Commission can reasonably argue that it is being asked, in effect, to back-date the application for benefit, which the regulations expressly prohibit unless there are exceptional circumstances. (See page 33.) If, on the other hand, the debt has accrued while the claimant was in receipt of benefit, and relates to a basic need such as rent, gas or electricity, payment of the debt by the Commission means that the need has been met twice over – once as part of the weekly benefit and once as an exceptional needs payment. This objection would not apply if the purpose for which the debt was incurred could be regarded as an exceptional need for which the Commission could have made an extra grant before the expenditure was undertaken; but even in these circumstances the Commission is reluctant to help, since the opportunity of verifying that the need was genuine and could not be met in any other way or at a lower cost may have been lost.

Despite these objections, the Commission will occasionally make a grant for the payment of a debt if, for example, there were good reasons for incurring the expense before asking for a grant, or if the existence of the debt itself constitutes an exceptional need because there is a danger of eviction or loss of basic amenities such as gas or electricity. When help of this kind is needed, however, it can often be obtained more readily from the social services department of the local authority, which can provide assistance to families where there is a risk of children having to be taken into the care of the local authority. Obviously this power can only be used if there are children in the family, though this restriction does not apply in Scotland. Local authorities vary widely in their readiness to provide such help. If they do so, it will normally be accompanied by a certain amount of supervision by a social worker, which some claimants may welcome but others will not. A lump-sum payment of this kind, whether made by the local authority, a charity or from any other source will not affect the claimant's weekly benefit entitlement.

Hire purchase

As we have already noted, the Commission is occasionally prepared to pay the balance of the purchase price of 'absolutely essential' furniture, rather than make a discretionary addition to meet the hire-purchase instalments as they fall due. See page 78.

Funeral expenses

When the national insurance death grant was introduced in 1949, the maximum payment was £20, and this was enough to pay for a simple funeral. The maximum death grant is now £30, which covers less than half the cost of a funeral. Paying for a funeral can therefore be a serious problem, especially if the only close relative of the dead person is a pensioner with no savings. The Supplementary Benefits Commission, however, is not normally prepared to make grants for this purpose. The reason for its reluctance is that local authorities have a duty, under section 50 of the National Assistance Act, 1948, to arrange for any person who has died in their area to be buried or cremated if it appears to them that no other suitable arrangements have been or are being made. The Commission takes the view that, if the relatives cannot afford to pay for a private funeral, the local authority should be asked to accept responsibility. As a funeral arranged by a local authority costs, on average, less than half as much as a private funeral, and the cost can be recovered subsequently out of the death grant (if any) or the estate of the deceased, the actual cost to the ratepayers is likely to be very small. The Commission's attitude, therefore, does not seem unreasonable.

There is, however, one major practical difficulty. The difference between a funeral arranged privately and one arranged (perhaps with the same undertaker) by a local authority may be small, but the difference in the way people feel about them is vast. To most people, a 'pauper burial' is the final indignity, to be avoided at all costs. Inevitably, therefore, private funerals are arranged by people who cannot afford to pay for them. Once the arrangements have been made, the local authority no longer has the power to accept responsibility for them or to meet the cost. The Commission will, therefore, consider making a grant to pay for a funeral after the debt has been incurred, if the person who has incurred it is receiving supplementary benefit or has an income only slightly above supplementary benefit level and is not in full-time work. Before making such a payment, the Handbook warns, 'the Commission must be satisfied that there are neither close relatives who could reasonably be expected to help with funeral expenses nor charitable funds available for this purpose'.

In these circumstances, it would obviously be unwise to assume that the Commission will agree to help with the cost of a funeral. The prudent course for anyone who cannot afford to pay for a private funeral is to approach the local authority with a view to having the funeral arranged by them. If this is not an acceptable solution, and help cannot be obtained from other sources, the alternative is to arrange the funeral privately, avoiding any unnecessary expenses, and apply to the social security office for an exceptional need payment *after* the funeral.

Emergencies

The Commission has virtually unlimited powers to provide help in an 'urgent case', whether the recipients would normally be eligible for supplementary benefit or not. This power, conferred by section 13 of the Ministry of Social Security Act, can for instance be used to help persons engaged in full-time work (see pages 182–3), or on strike (see pages 126–7). It is mainly used where a sudden catastrophe such as fire or flood has occurred, and the help given can include exceptional needs payments for the replacement of essential clothing and household equipment. Help can also be given under this section to a person in urgent need of money because of the loss or theft of a wallet or purse or of a wage packet.

Holidays

The types of exceptional needs payments described above are all mentioned in the *Handbook*, from which much of the information is taken. The *Handbook*, however, does not mention payments towards the cost of holidays, for the simple reason that the Commission refuses to make such payments. This does not mean, of course, that supplementary benefit recipients are not allowed to go away for holidays. They have as much right to do so as anybody else, subject only to the condition that a claimant who is normally required to register for work as a condition of payment of benefit must show that while away from home he is still available for work. Any extra expense involved in going away, however, will have to be met out of the normal weekly benefit, or out of savings, unless help can be obtained from some other source. Cheap or free holidays for old people, children, the handicapped and convalescents are arranged by local authorities, the Red Cross, the WRVS and various other bodies, and payment of supplementary benefit normally continues at the usual rate during short absences of this kind.

The situation regarding claimants who go abroad for a holiday, or for other reasons, is explained on pages 177–8.

Chapter 5

BELOW THE MINIMUM

The title of this chapter may seem like a contradiction, but the fact is that, while the supplementary benefit scale *is* a minimum so far as supplementary pensioners are concerned, for those below pension age, and especially for unemployed men, there are a number of possible reasons why, in a particular case, benefit may be reduced below the normal scale rates or withheld altogether – the wage stop, the special provisions relating to strikers, and the Commission's discretionary power to reduce benefit where there are exceptional circumstances, used mainly in cases where voluntary unemployment is suspected. Each of these will be considered in detail in this chapter. Another reason already mentioned in Chapter 2, and which can also affect pensioners (though it seldom does), is the 'unreasonable rent' rule (see pages 43–8).

The decision to reduce an individual's or a family's income below the usual guaranteed level must always be difficult, if not dangerous. Even when it is considered right to do so in the public interest, there is always a risk of serious hardship being caused to those directly concerned. Yet such decisions are being taken in many thousands of cases each day. Some of those decisions are undoubtedly wrong. A very large number of them would be reversed by an appeal tribunal if the facts were fully and fairly presented to it. The number of appeals lodged, however, is a very small proportion of the cases in which benefit is reduced or withheld, and few of those appealing have any skilled advice or assistance in presenting their case to the tribunal. There can be no doubt that, at any given time, thousands of individuals and families are living below the official poverty line because they are unaware of their rights or unable to assert them. The importance of the questions discussed in this chapter cannot, therefore, be over-emphasized.

THE WAGE STOP

It is a fundamental principle of the supplementary benefit scheme that an unemployed person should not be better off than he would be if working full-time in his normal occupation. If his supplementary benefit, worked out in the normal way, would raise his income above what he would get in full-time work, it is reduced accordingly and in some cases eliminated altogether. This rule, now embodied in paragraph 5 of schedule 2 of the Ministry of Social Security Act, goes back to the beginnings of unemployment assistance in 1935. The main difference between the present rule and its 1935 equivalent is that in 1935 the unemployed person's income was reduced *below* his normal earnings, whereas now it is only required that he should not be better off out of work.

It is important to distinguish between cases in which the wage stop *must* be applied unless there are 'exceptional circumstances', cases in which it *may* be applied at the Commission's discretion, and cases in which it must *not* be applied. The first category comprises claimants who are required to register for employment as a condition of receiving benefit – the unemployed. (See pages 28–9.) The second – those to whom the wage stop need not be applied – consists of claimants whom, 'by reason only of temporary circumstances', it would not be appropriate to require to register for employment – mainly people who are temporarily sick. The third category, to whom the wage stop must not be applied, consists of cases in which, for reasons which are not of a temporary nature, the requirement to register for work would be inappropriate – mainly women with dependent children, the chronically sick and the severely disabled. A mother claiming benefit while her husband is in prison falls into this third category, but may nevertheless have her benefit reduced, not under the wage stop as such but under the Commission's discretionary power to reduce benefit where there are exceptional circumstances. (See page 24.) Precisely where the lines should be drawn between the three categories is a matter of judgement, and the Commission's policy on this point is discussed more fully in the following pages.

The effect of the wage stop, in those cases to which it does apply, can be illustrated by a simple example:

Richard B., an unemployed man, is married with four children. The family's requirements, according to the supplementary benefit scale, including rent, amount to £25 per week. Their resources consist of unemployment benefit £16·40, family allowance £2·90, and family income supplement (FIS) 60p, making a total of £19·90. His normal supplementary benefit assessment would be:

Requirements	£25·00
Less resources	19·90
Supplementary allowance	5·10

But his full-time earnings when working in his normal occupation are only £22 gross, from which national insurance contributions and fares to work must be deducted, leaving net earnings of £19·50. To ensure that he is not better off out of work, his unemployment benefit and supplementary benefit, added together, must not exceed this figure. His supplementary allowance must therefore be reduced to £3·10 (£19·50 less £16·40). This is £2 less than his normal entitlement.

In this example we have assumed that Richard B., when in full-time work, claimed family income supplement, which, being awarded for a period of twenty-six weeks, would continue in payment when he became unemployed. If he had not claimed FIS, it would still be taken into account in calculating the maximum benefit he could receive under the wage-stop rule. The reason for this is that the wage stop is intended to prevent him from being better off out of work than he will be when he goes back to work. The comparison that must be made is between his income as it is now and as it would be if he were now to recommence full-time work. The fact that he did not claim FIS in the past is irrelevant, since it must be assumed that, having been informed of his entitlement, he will claim it as soon as he is in full-time employment again (FIS can only be claimed by persons in full-time work; see pages 188–9). The figures will now be as follows:

Requirements (as above): £25. Resources: unemployment benefit £16·40, and family allowance £2·90 – total £19·30. Supplementary allowance (before wage-stop deduction): £5·70. Maximum benefit (unemployment benefit and supplementary allowance combined) is arrived at by adding FIS (60p) to the normal net earnings figure of £19·50. The supplementary allowance actually payable will therefore be £3·70 (£20·10 less unemployment benefit of £16·40) – £2 below his normal entitlement, as before.

If these calculations seem confusing, the principle to bear in mind is that *the family's income from all sources when the claimant is out of work must not be more than its income from all sources (including FIS where appropriate) when he is in work.*

If the claimant is doing a part-time job while drawing benefit, the effect on the wage-stop calculation depends on whether it is a job that he can do only while unemployed or whether he will be able to continue doing it when back in full-time work. In either case the principle is the same – that his total income while out of work must not exceed his total income when in work. All but £1 of the part-time earnings will be taken into account in calculating the normal amount of benefit that would be payable but for the wage stop; but the amount of benefit actually payable under the wage stop will not be affected unless the part-time earnings must cease when the claimant returns to full-time work. In that case, they will be taken into account in full, in precisely the same way as unemployment benefit, in comparing his income while unemployed with the income he can expect to get when in work.

The main problem in administering the wage stop is to decide what would be the claimant's 'net weekly earnings if he were engaged in full-time work in his normal occupation'. The first question to be answered is: what is his normal occupation? Having settled that point, the Commission has

to decide what would be his net earnings if he were now working full-time in that occupation, and this involves two further
questions: what is meant by 'net earnings', and how is 'full-
time work' to be defined? Each of these questions must now
be considered.

Normal occupation

The Commission generally assumes that the type of work for
which a claimant is registered at the employment exchange is
his normal occupation. In most cases this assumption is
correct; but not in all. If a claimant has worked for years at
the same job, is still able to do this kind of work, and can be
expected to find a job of this kind in the near future, there will
not be much doubt what his normal occupation is. But very
few wage-stop cases are as simple as that. If a man has had
more than one occupation, it may be difficult to say which one
is 'normal'. A skilled man who temporarily resorts to less
skilled work rather than remain unemployed does not thereby
change his normal occupation; but if the reason for the change
is that his skill is no longer wanted by employers, the Commission may argue that his normal occupation is that of an
unskilled labourer even if he has never done labouring work,
simply because that is the only kind of work he is likely to get.
Similarly, if a man who is recovering from an illness or an
injury is forced temporarily to seek work at a lower wage
than he would normally receive, this temporary work does not
become his normal occupation; but if he is unlikely to recover
sufficiently to return to his old job, the Commission can
reasonably argue that his normal occupation has changed and
that the wage stop should be based on his present reduced
earning capacity, or at best on the kind of job he can expect
to get in the future, after retraining.

For most of those affected by the wage stop, however,
'normal occupation' has little meaning. They have no special
skills, and have often done a variety of jobs for varying
lengths of time and at varying wage rates. Many of them are

in some degree disabled and have been unemployed for considerable periods. They are probably registered at the employment exchange as 'labourer' or, if they are not capable of heavy manual work, as 'light labourer'. These terms cover a wide assortment of jobs, some (at least in the 'labourer' category) relatively well paid and others very badly. For cases of this sort, where it is impossible to arrive at a precise estimate of the individual's probable earnings in full-time work, a new policy was laid down by the Commission in 1967, in a report entitled *Administration of the Wage Stop*:

The Commission have decided that in future the wage fixed by the National Joint Council for Local Authorities (Manual Workers) should be used as a reasonable measure of earnings for those claimants for whom it is not possible to take either an individual earnings figure or the standard earnings figure for a particular industry in a particular locality . . . Where the general rates of earnings prevailing in a Region, or part of a Region, are clearly substantially higher, a higher rate may be authorized.

Whether local authority wage rates will provide a reasonable basis for estimating the earning capacity of a particular claimant depends not only on the kind of work he is qualified to do, but also on the way in which, from the basic wage rates, 'net earnings for full-time work' are calculated.

Net earnings for full-time work

Once a decision has been made as to the claimant's normal occupation, the next stage is to estimate how much he would earn working full-time in that occupation. The relevant figure is not the basic wage rate but the amount that he would actually bring home at the end of the week. This may include overtime, bonuses and commission (if these are not paid weekly, an average weekly figure must be estimated; and, similarly, a monthly salary must be expressed as so much per week). From the total gross wage, the regulations provide that there shall be deducted

(a) any sum the deduction of which from salary or wages is authorized by statute; and

(b) any expenses reasonably incurred by him in connexion with his employment.

In practice, the deductions usually made are for income tax, national insurance contributions and fares to work. The 1967 report announced that, in future, no deduction was to be made for 'expenses such as the extra cost of meals out and wear and tear on clothes', since these expenses did not result entirely from the man's employment.

For the purposes of the wage stop, it is to the claimant's advantage that his potential earnings should be assessed at as high a figure as can reasonably be justified. The basic rate for the job may be found to vary among local employers. The rate earned by the claimant when in work may provide reasonable evidence of what he is likely to earn when he returns to work. Otherwise, the fairest figure to take may be the rate offered by the largest employer of this type of labour in the locality. Whatever basic rate is adopted, it is important to ensure that adequate allowance is made for overtime and other extra payments. Since overtime is usually a variable item, this inevitably introduces an element of uncertainty into the calculation. Evidence should be obtained from trade unions, employers or other sources as to the amount of overtime currently being worked in the occupation in question – or, if overtime has been temporarily reduced because of bad weather, strikes, etc., the amount normally worked.

Where, in the absence of precise evidence of the claimant's earning capacity, National Joint Council (NJC) wage rates for local authority manual workers are used, the Commission takes the basic wage rate for a forty-hour week as the claimant's normal gross earnings, from which deductions are made for national insurance contributions and fares to work in order to arrive at an estimate of net earnings. On this basis, the *gross* earnings figures are as in Table 6 (up-to-date figures can be obtained from the local employment exchange, council offices or the National Union of General and Municipal

TABLE 6: WAGES RATES INTRODUCED AS FROM NOVEMBER
1971

Labourers (Grade 'B') – London		£19·90
	Elsewhere	£17·90
Light labourers (Grade 'A') – London		£19·45
	Elsewhere	£17·45

Workers). These figures, however, are not a true measure of
what the claimant could expect to earn if he were to get a job
with the local council. Council employees in these grades now
enjoy a minimum-earnings guarantee which ensures that, for
a full week's work, their wages do not fall below £21 in
London and £19 in other parts of the country (at November
1971 wage rates). Actual earnings are in many cases higher
than this because of overtime. Neither the minimum-earnings
guarantee nor overtime earnings are taken into account by
the Commission in cases where the NJC rates are used as a
basis for estimating potential earnings, although it is the normal practice to take probable overtime earnings into account
in other cases. It is true that the NJC rates cover a wide
variety of jobs and it is seldom possible to say exactly how
much overtime a particular claimant would be likely to work;
but that is not a good reason for assuming that he would do
no overtime at all, and still less for ignoring the minimum-
earnings guarantee.

The average working week for manual workers in local
government employment in October 1971, according to the
Department of Employment's earnings survey, was 43·4
hours. As this average includes men who worked less than a
full week because of sickness, it is probably fair to take four
hours as the average amount of overtime worked, ignoring
seasonal variations. The overtime rates are time-and-a-third
for the first two hours of weekday overtime, time-and-a-half
for other weekday overtime and Saturday work, and double
time for Sundays. On the basis of the national figures, therefore, at least £2·50 should be added to the basic wage to arrive
at the normal earnings figure for the purpose of the wage
stop. This should normally be regarded as a minimum, but it

is worth inquiring about the earnings of local authority labourers in the particular locality concerned. The amount of overtime being worked locally may be above the national average. Many local authorities operate incentive bonus schemes and a few pay higher basic rates than those laid down by the National Joint Council. All these factors must be taken into account in deciding what the claimant's 'net earnings for full-time work' would be if he were employed as a local authority labourer or light labourer. The light labourer classification should be adopted only if, because of a permanent physical disability, he is plainly unable to do heavy manual work.

The figure arrived at in this way will generally be a good deal higher than the Commission's estimate of normal earnings, but it still may not provide a fair indication of the claimant's earning capacity. Although the NJC hourly wage rates compare favourably with those of most unskilled workers, the *weekly* earnings of local authority workers are low in comparison with those in many other industries. Again, evidence should be obtained about the earnings of unskilled workers employed by large firms in the locality.

Care should be taken also to ensure that the deductions made to arrive at net weekly earnings are not excessive. The question of income tax liability will not usually arise and national insurance contributions should cause no difficulty (if necessary, the local national insurance office of the Department of Health and Social Security will confirm the total weekly contribution, flat-rate and graduated, payable on a given amount of gross earnings). The deduction made for fares to work, if any, can only be a rough estimate since the exact place of work cannot be predicted with any certainty. Usually the estimate is, if anything, on the low side, which operates to the claimant's advantage, but it should always be checked, especially if the claimant is in the habit of going to work by bicycle or other means which involve little or no expense.

Discussion of normal earnings with claimant

One of the changes announced in the 1967 report, *Administra-tion of the Wage Stop*, was that

in every case where a wage-stop deduction is being considered there should be discussion with the claimant about his normal earnings and about the amount to be deducted for expenses. As it will not usually be possible to settle these matters at the initial visit, the notification subsequently issued to the claimant about the amount of his Supplementary Benefit, if the wage stop is applied, will state explicitly the net earnings figure taken for assessment purposes and the amount by which the Supplementary Benefit has been reduced below the normal entitlement.

It is important that this procedure should be carried out. In the event of the wage stop being applied without prior dis-cussion of the claimant's normal earnings, or if the earnings figure on which it is based is not in accordance with the information given by the claimant, he should take the matter up at once and, if necessary, appeal.

It is equally important that, before the discussion of the claimant's normal earnings, the precise meaning of this term should be explained to him; in particular, the fact that it must be based on his normal occupation, that it is present earning capacity that counts rather than past earnings (though past earnings can of course be used as evidence), that any tem-porary disability should be discounted, and that a realistic figure of overtime should be included if appropriate. This is not done at present, with the result that the claimant's benefit is often based on an estimate of normal earnings arrived at with his agreement but not in accordance with the require-ments of the Ministry of Social Security Act. If the claimant becomes aware that his earning capacity has been under-estimated for this reason, he should insist on the question being re-opened, and arrears should be paid if a higher earn-ings figure is agreed. Refusal to review the original decision constitutes grounds for an appeal.

Similarly, it may well happen that the claimant is himself

uncertain of his probable future earnings at the point when the question is discussed with him. Subsequent inquiries may show that the figure he then accepted as reasonable is in fact too low. The Commission should be asked to reconsider the matter in the light of the new evidence and to pay arrears if appropriate.

Adjustment of the wage-stop figure

Since the wage stop is based on the claimant's earning capacity in his normal occupation, it will be affected by any increase in the level of earnings in the occupation in question. The Commission's policy, laid down in the 1967 report on the wage stop, is 'to maintain a continuing review of earnings rates, with a view to giving effect to any earnings increase as it occurs'. Nevertheless, there is often some delay between a wage increase and the adjustment of supplementary allowances to take account of it. When such delays occur, arrears of benefit should always be paid. If the pay award is itself back-dated, the arrears of benefit should go back to the same date as the pay increase. Former claimants who have gone back to work and are no longer in receipt of benefit may find themselves entitled to arrears of benefit due to a pay increase, but arrears are unlikely to be paid in these circumstances unless actually requested (if the wage stop was based on NJC rates, arrears are, in theory, paid automatically in such cases, but this may not always happen in practice).

Any increases in NJC wage rates will be taken into account by the Commission, and wage-stop assessments based on those rates should be adjusted accordingly, without any prompting by the claimants concerned, though there is sometimes considerable delay. Other pay increases affecting wage-stopped claimants may go unnoticed for several months unless the claimants themselves draw attention to them.

In some cases the Commission's estimate of the claimant's potential earnings is revised downwards rather than upwards. This is liable to occur where a man has been unemployed for some time and it is considered unlikely that he will find work in what was previously regarded as his 'normal occupation'. He is therefore reclassified by the employment exchange, probably as a labourer. If adjustment to the level of earnings appropriate to the new 'normal occupation' involves a reduction in benefit of more than 50p, the reduction is made by instalments of 50p every four weeks until the new level is reached, under the Commission's general powers to exercise discretion where there are exceptional circumstances. Claimants who are reclassified in this way should always consider very carefully whether the Commission's action is justified, and, if in doubt, they should appeal against the reduction of benefit.

Claimants affected by the wage stop

In addition to the general points discussed above, there are a number of other points to be noted regarding the application of the wage stop to particular categories of claimants.

(a) *Unemployed men.* The wage stop must be applied to claimants who are required to register for work as a condition of receiving benefit, unless there are exceptional circumstances. The requirement to register for work is normally imposed, under section 11 of the Ministry of Social Security Act, on claimants under pension age who are unemployed but are not prevented from working by sickness or the need to care for children or other dependants. (See pages 28–9.) A claimant who is disabled but has not been certified by a doctor as unfit for work will normally be expected to register for work, and the wage stop will be applied to him in the same way as to anybody else: if payment of benefit in full would make him better off than when working full-time in his normal occupation, his benefit will be reduced accordingly. Since the earning capacity of a disabled person may be extremely low, he is actually more likely to be wage-stopped than an able-bodied person in similar circumstances and the reduction in his benefit may, in extreme cases, amount to several pounds per week. Unfair as this may seem, it is a logical consequence of the wage-stop rule that those with the smallest earning capacity should receive the smallest amount of benefit when not working.

Similarly, the wage stop is more likely to affect those with large families, especially if they have teen-age children: not because their earning capacity is abnormally low (though this may also be true) but because, even with the family income supplement, less help is given by the state towards the cost of children when the head of the family is in work than when he is unemployed.

There are two ways in which an unemployed person can be exempted from the operation of the wage stop. The first is for the Commission to waive the requirement to register for employment. The second is to show that there are exceptional circumstances.

The Commission recognizes that there are cases of severe disablement in which no real purpose is served by requiring registration for work, and the requirement is occasionally waived on these grounds. This does not prevent the disabled person from continuing to register at the employment exchange if he wishes to do so, but it does mean that the wage stop need not be applied to him. In the case of blind persons, the possibility of waiving the requirement to register is automatically considered if they have been continuously unemployed for two years.

The Commission also recognizes the existence of a certain number of men who are 'virtually unemployable' through 'a combination of disability, age, length of unemployment, etc.'. In such cases, even if registration is still required (as it normally is, at least once a quarter, unless the man is 'accepted as incapable of work'), the wage stop is removed on the grounds that there are exceptional circumstances. Apart from cases of this sort, which are rare, the Commission does not make use of the 'exceptional circumstances' loophole to exempt unemployed men from the operation of the wage stop.

What it does occasionally do is to 'add back' part of the wage-stop deduction – i.e. to allow the man to receive a bigger income than he would have when in work, but less than the full rate of benefit to which he would be entitled but for the wage stop. This is done where it is felt that hardship would result from the rigid application of the wage stop. It is a somewhat illogical compromise and there is even some doubt as to its legality, since the wording of the Act appears to mean that the wage stop should be applied rigorously unless there are exceptional circumstances, in which case it should not be applied at all. Adherence to the letter of the law, however, might well result in greater hardship, so it is probably best to turn a blind eye to the vagaries of the Commission in this instance.

It must, however, be stressed that the Commission could, if it wished, administer the wage-stop rule far more liberally. It is not obliged to require any claimant to register for employment and, therefore, it can always avoid applying the wage stop if it wishes to do so. A more practical possibility is that 'exceptional circumstances' could be interpreted far more broadly. A clear precedent is to be found in the annual report for 1937 of the Commission's predecessor, the Unemployment Assistance Board:

> The Board have instructed their officers that a family of five or more children may in itself be regarded as a sufficient departure from the normal to justify consideration of waiving or mitigating the application of the wages stop on the ground of 'special circumstances'.

The UAB was clearly worried about the hardship that could be caused by compelling families to live below the normal minimum income level for long periods of time, and anxious to avoid applying the wage stop wherever it reasonably could. The Commission seems determined to apply it rigidly unless there are overwhelming reasons for *not* doing so. It should be urged to use its discretion more liberally in any case where the claimant has a large family, or there is a sick or disabled person in the household, or employment prospects are particularly poor – in short, wherever exceptional circumstances can be said to exist. If the Commission refuses, the appeal tribunal may well take a more sympathetic view.

(b) *Temporarily sick men.* It may seem odd that the wage stop should be applied to men for whom the possibility of employment does not exist because a doctor has certified them as unfit for work. The Commission is in fact allowed to apply the wage stop in such cases only if the sickness is of a temporary nature, and even then the Act only says that the wage stop *may* be applied. The 1967 report justifies wage-stopping the sick by arguing that 'it would be anomalous ... if a man were paid more than he could earn, when he was likely to be working, or fit for work again, very soon'.

In practice, the Commission's official policy is not to apply the wage stop where the illness has lasted, or is expected to last, for three months or more. It is, however, applied in cases where the claimant is expected to be fit for work within three months, in precisely the same way as if he were unemployed. If the wage stop is applied at the outset and it later becomes clear that the illness is likely to last three months or more, the wage stop will then be removed, but arrears are not paid for the period during which benefit has been reduced. It is important, therefore, to ensure that, if the illness is likely to be of a long-term nature, it is treated as such from the start. The doctor should be asked for a note to this effect, since, as the *Handbook* explains, 'If the position is doubtful ... the wage stop, if appropriate, is to be applied'.

Even if the illness is certain to be of short duration, the wage stop is entirely discretionary. If there is any question of hardship being caused, the Commission should be asked to pay benefit in full on these grounds. Often the illness will result in additional expense for the family, and this should be taken into account by the Commission in deciding whether the wage stop should be applied. Even if there are no obvious exceptional circumstances, an appeal tribunal may take the view that it is wrong in principle that a man who is genuinely sick should have his benefit reduced in this way.

(c) *Temporarily absent husbands.* Women with children who claim supplementary benefit are not subject to the wage stop, since they are not regarded as being in a position to take employment. A deduction on the lines of the wage stop may, however, be applied to a woman whose husband is temporarily absent – usually in prison, but it has been known for cases of desertion to be treated in the same way if the husband is expected to return. The woman's benefit is limited by reference not to her own earning capacity but to that of her husband, the reason given by the *Handbook* being that 'it would be anomalous, and contrary to the general principle underlying the wage stop, if a family's income were increased during the short-term absence of the husband so that it was more than the benefit payable when he was at home, and more than he could earn'.

As in the case of sickness, whether the deduction is applied or not depends on how long the situation is expected to continue. If the husband is serving a prison sentence of three months or less (including time spent in custody pending trial or appeal and ignoring possible remission for good conduct), the wife's benefit will not be allowed to exceed the husband's normal full-time earnings. If he is expected to remain in custody for more than three months, the wife will receive benefit at the full rate, even if this results in her being better off financially during her husband's absence.

The restriction of benefit in this way during the absence of the breadwinner, under the Commission's discretionary power to reduce benefit where there are exceptional circumstances, has never been approved or even discussed by Parliament. Although the Commission may argue that it would be anomalous to pay benefit at the normal rate in such cases, it is equally anomalous to apply the wage stop in circumstances where the possibility of employment does not exist.

Rent and rate rebates

In cases where benefit is reduced because of the wage stop, it is particularly important that the claimant should obtain any other benefits and rebates to which he may be entitled. Rate rebates are not normally given to supplementary benefit recipients, because their weekly benefit includes an allowance for rent and rates. The effect of the wage stop, however, is that benefit is no longer based on the family's needs, including rent and rates, but on the claimant's earning capacity; and it will therefore not be affected by a reduction of rent or rates. Accordingly, wage-stopped claimants (and certain others; see page 57) should receive from the social security office a special application form to be forwarded to the local council offices if it appears that they may be entitled to a rate rebate. It is often found that this form has not been issued, with the result that a rebate has been lost (a rate rebate cannot be granted unless it was claimed before the end of the six-month period to which it relates). The Commission has instructed its officers that, where this has occurred, special consideration should be given to the possibility of making a lump-sum grant for any exceptional needs that may exist.

The special method of calculating a rent rebate or allowance under the Housing Finance Act for a tenant receiving supplementary benefit for more than eight weeks does not apply to claimants who are subject to the wage stop. Instead the normal formula laid down in schedule 3 to the Housing Finance Act is used, the rent rebate or allowance being based on the claimant's normal income when in full-time work, as estimated for the purposes of the wage stop. If this estimate is correct, he will receive the same rent rebate or allowance when out of work as he is entitled to in full-time work.

Exceptional needs payments

If the Commission feels obliged, because of the wage-stop rule, to reduce a family's income below the normal minimum standard represented by the scale rates, it has a particular responsibility for ensuring that full use is made of its discretionary powers to give additional help in the form of lump-sum grants to meet specific needs. (See pages 85–107.)

STRIKES AND OTHER TRADE DISPUTES

Claimants who are wage-stopped should not hesitate to ask for such grants to meet any major items of expenditure of an essential nature, especially if they have been in receipt of benefit at a reduced rate for several months.

STRIKES AND OTHER TRADE DISPUTES

There are special rules regarding the entitlement to supplementary benefit of persons who are on strike or who are without work as a result of a 'stoppage of work due to a trade dispute' (a term which covers both strikes and lock-outs). The main provision relating to trade disputes is to be found in section 10 of the Ministry of Social Security Act, 1966, which states that a person who is without employment because of such a stoppage at his place of employment is to have his own requirements disregarded for supplementary benefit purposes. This restriction, however, does not apply if he can prove *both*

(a) 'that he is not participating in or financing or directly interested in the trade dispute which caused the stoppage of work'; and

(b) 'that he does not belong to a grade or class of workers of which, immediately before the commencement of the stoppage, there were members employed at his place of employment any of whom are participating in or financing or directly interested in the dispute'.

Section 10 is modelled on section 22(1) of the National Insurance Act, 1965, which provides that, with similar exceptions, a person who has lost employment by reason of a stoppage of work due to a trade dispute at his place of employment shall be disqualified from receiving unemployment benefit. Because of the similarity of these provisions, section 18(2) of the Ministry of Social Security Act provides that, where a supplementary benefit appeal involves a question as to whether a person's requirements should be disregarded under section 10, this question is to be referred to the national insurance tribunal.

There is a considerable body of national insurance case law

on the meaning, in this context, of such terms as 'participating in', 'financing', 'directly interested in' and 'grade or class of workers'. Many of the leading cases decided by the National Insurance Commissioners are reported in the *Digest of Commissioners' Decisions*, a copy of which can be consulted at the local national insurance office, and strikers should be able to obtain advice on legal questions of this kind through their trade union. Generally speaking, however, it can be assumed that, in the event of a strike, anybody employed at the same workplace whose pay or conditions of employment are likely to be affected by the outcome of the dispute or who is a member of a union which is supporting some of the strikers financially, will be caught by section 10. The fact that a particular worker may be opposed to the strike and has done everything in his power to prevent it is no protection. Even if he is not a member of the union and has no interest in the outcome, he may still fall within the provisions of section 10 if any other worker in the same 'grade or class' as himself is 'participating in or financing or directly interested in the dispute'. And it should be noted that section 10 places on the individual concerned the onus of proving that neither he nor anybody in the same grade or class is involved in the dispute.

Once it is established that the case is one to which section 10 applies, the effect is that, if the claimant is a single person with no children, his requirements are disregarded and there can therefore be no entitlement to supplementary benefit, except in a case of urgent need where payments can be made under section 13. (See page 106.) During the 1972 miners' strike, the Commission issued a statement explaining how its officers were instructed to interpret section 13 in relation to single strikers:

. . . no payment is made to a single person in lodgings unless he can satisfy the officer that he will be evicted straight away if he cannot pay his landlady; and no payments are to be made where a single person lives with his parents unless the parents themselves are in poor circumstances, for example if they are living on supplementary benefit. If a single person lives alone, it will be accepted more readily that he may need money to buy food. If the officer decides to make a payment of supplementary benefit he will bring the person's other resources (including any available capital) up to the level which he considers necessary in the circumstances. In no case, however, is this level to exceed £4 and it may well be less than this.

The £4 limit is of course subject to adjustment from time to time, and can be exceeded in individual cases where there is an urgent need of more than £4, since it is not laid down in the Act but is merely an expression of the Commission's normal policy.

The treatment of strikers with dependants is different from that of single strikers. Only the requirements of the striker himself are excluded by section 10, and benefit can still be paid to meet the needs of his wife and children. The wife's requirements are assessed by the method prescribed for this purpose in paragraph 14 of schedule 2 of the Act, taking the appropriate scale rate for a 'non-householder' and adding the normal allowance for rent (i.e., in most cases, the full net weekly rent); and the normal scale rates for the children are added. The same method of calculation would be used in the less usual situation where the claimant's wife, rather than the claimant himself, was involved in a trade dispute; his requirements would be assessed as if he were a single 'non-householder', while those of his wife would be disregarded. In the case of a single man or woman with dependent children, or a couple who are both out of work because of a trade dispute, only the requirements of the children would be taken into account, though a full allowance for the rent would still be added. In cases of this sort, however, additional payments are sometimes made under section 13 on grounds of urgent need.

Under the procedure described above, where section 10 applies, the normal supplementary benefit entitlement, at present rates of benefit, is reduced by £5·45 in the case of a married couple one of whom is caught by its provisions, and by £6·55 in the case of a single householder with children;

while single childless claimants, and childless couples where both husband and wife are involved in trade disputes, lose the whole of their entitlement, whatever it would otherwise be (the figures given here take no account of section 13 payments, nor of the effect of the special rules regarding the treatment of resources in trade dispute cases, described below). In the former type of case, where benefit can be paid to meet the needs of dependants, there may be a possibility of mitigating the effect of section 10 by means of additional allowances on grounds of exceptional circumstances (see Chapter 4); but such allowances cannot be paid for the purpose of meeting any special needs of the person involved in the trade dispute, since his requirements must be disregarded. In the latter type of case, since there are no dependants whose requirements can be taken into account, the possibility of an exceptional circumstances addition does not arise. The Commission's power to make payments under section 13 in an urgent case should, however, be kept in mind, especially if the dispute is prolonged and there is a risk of serious hardship.

Local social security offices faced with demands for help from single strikers who are disqualified under section 10 have been known to compromise by offering an advance rather than an outright grant of benefit, or even asking the claimant to sign an undertaking to repay the money. Since the Commission has no power to make benefit recoverable – except in an urgent case where the claimant is in full-time work (see pages 182–3) or where benefit is paid on return to work after a strike (see pages 130–32) – an undertaking of this kind cannot be enforced and ought not to be demanded. Once satisfied that urgent need exists, the Commission should meet it by an outright grant, and normally does so. A claimant who has been prevailed upon to sign an undertaking to repay and later realizes that he should not have been asked to do so should inform the local office of its error and make it clear that he does not regard the undertaking as binding.

The treatment of resources

In calculating the amount of benefit payable to a striker or other person involved in a trade dispute, although his own requirements may have to be disregarded under section 10, his resources and those of his dependants, including any strike pay or similar payments, must be taken into account. The normal 'disregards' apply (see Chapter 3), except that PAYE tax refunds are treated as income rather than savings and taken into account in full, subject only to the overall disregard of the first £1 per week of 'other income'. (See pages 64–5.) Prior to November 1971, a more generous procedure was followed, whereby a striker's resources were disregarded to the extent necessary to meet his own requirements. The Social Security Act, 1971, put an end to this by requiring that tax refunds and strike pay be taken into account as income subject to the £1 disregard. The treatment of tax refunds as income applies not only where the recipient is regarded as being involved in a trade dispute for the purposes of section 10 of the Ministry of Social Security Act, but in any case where the tax refund is not 'attributable to any period of absence from work through sickness or other similar cause or to any period of unemployment'. Thus any claimant who is still in employment but laid off temporarily owing to a trade dispute in whose financing or outcome he may have no stake whatsoever will still have any tax refund taken into account as income for supplementary benefit purposes under the provisions of the 1971 Act.

An obvious way to avoid having a tax refund taken into account, one might think, would be simply not to claim it until the strike is over. The 1971 Act, however, closes this loophole by providing that not only tax refunds actually paid but also any refund which becomes available or would become available if applied for are to be treated as income. In some strikes, tax refunds are *not* available because the clerical staff who would pay them are also involved in the dispute and it has not been possible to arrange for the refunds to be paid directly from the local tax offices rather than through the employer. The result is that any refunds due are paid in a lump sum at the end of the strike and are then taken into account (subject to the usual £1 disregard) in calculating the benefit, if any, payable for the first fifteen days after resumption of work (see below).

Returning to work after a trade dispute

Supplementary benefit can be paid for up to fifteen days after a return to work, just as it can after a period of unemployment or sickness. (See pages 183–5.) Once the stoppage of work due to the trade dispute is over, section 10 no longer applies, and the requirements of a person involved in the dispute can then be taken into account in the normal way. This means that a single person, who cannot normally claim benefit during a strike, can claim during the fifteen days following the end of the strike. The right to benefit on a return to work after a trade dispute is, however, subject to special rules.

The first of these rules applies to anybody returning to work after a stoppage due to a trade dispute, whether subject to section 10 (i.e. involved in some way in the dispute) or not. Any earnings received during the first fifteen days are to be taken into account in full, without deducting the usual 'disregard' of £1. Moreover, any advance of earnings *made or offered* during that period is also to be taken into account in full. The object of this rule is to ensure that, so far as possible, on a return to work after a strike, the strikers look to the employer rather than to the social security system for any help they may need to tide them over until the next pay-day.

The second special rule, operating from April 1972, applies only to those who, during the stoppage of work, fell within the provisions of section 10. Any supplementary benefit paid to them during the first fifteen days after their return to work is recoverable, normally through the employer. This rule is laid down in section 2 of the Social Security Act, 1971, and the provisions regarding the method of recovery are set out in schedule 1 of that Act. The Commission, on making a payment of benefit in these circumstances, must supply to the claimant and to the Secretary of State for Social Services a 'notification of award', showing the amount of benefit and the claimant's 'protected earnings', i.e. the amount below which his net weekly earnings, after the usual deductions, are not to be further reduced by the recovery of benefit. The protected earnings figure is calculated by taking the claimant's requirements according to the supplementary benefit scale, adding £3 and subtracting any family allowances.

On receiving a notification of award under section 2 of the 1971 Act, the Secretary of State must serve a 'deduction notice' on the employer, showing the amount of benefit to be recovered (after deducting any amount that has already been repaid) and the claimant's protected earnings. A deduction notice remains valid for up to fourteen weeks, after which, if the benefit has not been recovered in full, a new deduction notice can be issued. The employer must proceed to deduct from the claimant's earnings each week one tenth of the total amount to be recovered, subject to the protected earnings figure (if the net earnings for a particular week are less than the protected earnings, no deduction can be made). The employer may deduct more than one tenth of the total amount each week, but only with the claimant's written consent. Once the total amount deducted by the employer is equal to the amount shown on the deduction notice, the notice lapses and no further deductions are to be made. The notice also lapses if the claimant leaves the employment of the employer on whom it was served, but the Secretary of State may serve a new deduction notice on the new employer, if any. The amount deductible each week by the new employer will be one tenth (or more if the employee agrees) of the amount then remaining to be recovered. If at any time recovery of benefit by means of a deduction notice is not practicable, the Secretary of State can use other means of recovery, including legal action; but it is unlikely that this would happen unless it was thought that the claimant was deliberately avoiding repayment.

The Social Security Act, 1971, made no provision for appeals in connection with the procedure for recovery of benefit under section 2. There is therefore no right of appeal to the local tribunal against a decision that benefit is recoverable, the amount to be recovered or the amount of protected earnings. If any such decision is not in accordance with the provisions of the Act, however, the claimant may be able to seek redress through the Courts and he should seek legal advice.

VOLUNTARY UNEMPLOYMENT

There are a number of ways in which the Commission discourages or prevents people who are fit and available for work from living in idleness at the taxpayers' expense. Although aimed at preventing *voluntary* idleness (or at least relieving the State of the cost of maintaining the voluntarily idle in their own homes), some of these measures affect large numbers of people who are out of work through no fault of their own.

Prosecution

Section 30 of the Ministry of Social Security Act, 1966, provides that if a person persistently refuses or neglects to maintain himself and his wife and children, and as a result supplementary benefit has to be paid in respect of any of them or free accommodation provided at a reception centre, he can be prosecuted. If convicted, he is liable to up to three months' imprisonment, a fine of up to £100, or both. Anybody faced with a prosecution under this section should at once obtain legal advice. Prosecution, however, is only used as a last resort when other methods of persuasion have failed, and is always preceded by an interview during which the claimant is warned of the possible consequences of his behaviour.

Re-establishment centres and training courses

Less extreme measures than prosecution are the offer of a place in a re-establishment centre in lieu of payment of a supplementary allowance, or the requirement that a claimant should attend a course of instruction or training as a condition of receiving benefit. The Commission may resort to these methods under section 12 of the Act, if they consider that a claimant is refusing or neglecting to maintain himself or his wife and children, but not if he is in receipt of unemployment benefit. The Commission cannot use its powers under section 12 without first obtaining a direction from the appeal tribunal that, for a specified period, the claimant shall be subject to the provisions of the section; and before making such a direction the tribunal must give the claimant an opportunity of stating his case. He can be represented at the hearing, in the same way as at any other hearing before the tribunal. (See pages 207–8.) Once the tribunal has made a direction, it is for the Commission to decide whether to make use of its powers and if so how.

In practice, the power to require attendance at a course of instruction or training is seldom, if ever, exercised, and the provisions of section 12 relating to re-establishment centres are used in only a small number of cases. There is a chronic shortage of training facilities and the Department of Employment would certainly not want them used as a penalty for voluntary idleness. As for the re-establishment centres, they are provided by the Commission itself and their purpose is explained in paragraph 1 of schedule 4 of the Ministry of Social Security Act:

For the re-establishment of persons in need thereof through lack of regular occupation or of instruction or training the Commission may provide centres, to be known as re-establishment centres, where (whether in consequence of a determination of the Commission under section 12 of this Act or otherwise) such persons may attend or may be maintained by the Commission, and in either case may be afforded by the Commission the occupation, instruction or training requisite to fit them for entry into or return to regular employment.

There are thirteen centres, three of which have residential facilities for men living at a distance. The usual period of attendance is up to about three months. The centres do not attempt to provide training in a particular skill but rather to help long-unemployed men (there are no centres for women) to re-acquire the habit of regular work. They vary in quality, but the best of them seem to achieve this aim in a considerable proportion of cases, if the number of men getting jobs on leaving the centres is any guide. The chances of success would obviously be reduced if the re-establishment centres were regarded as penal institutions, and the Commission attaches a great deal of importance to the fact that most of the men attending them do so voluntarily rather than as the result of a direction under section 12 – though it is probably also true that many of the 'voluntary' attenders are aware that their benefit might have been cut off if they had refused to go.

While attending a re-establishment centre under a section 12 direction, the claimant is entitled to such payments as the Commission thinks fit, to meet his personal requirements or those of his dependants. In practice, no distinction is made between section 12 cases and those attending voluntarily. If living at home, they normally receive payments at the same rate as the supplementary allowance they were receiving previously, plus an allowance for travelling expenses where necessary. A man who is being maintained at a residential re-establishment centre gets an allowance for his personal expenses, while his family receives an allowance calculated in the same way as if he were permanently absent.

Reduction of benefit

The Social Security Act, 1971, introduced a new rule under which a claimant who is himself responsible for the fact that he is unemployed has his supplementary allowance reduced by 40 per cent of the appropriate scale rate for a single person.

The 40 per cent reduction, based on the scale rates which came into force in October 1972, comes to £2·60 for a married man or a single householder. For a single person who is a 'non-householder', the reduction is £2·05 for those aged 18 or over and £1·60 for those under 18. Whenever the scale rates are increased, each of these figures will increase to 40 per cent of the new rates. The 1971 Act does not specify the reduction to be made in the case of a claimant who pays an inclusive sum for board and lodging, but the Commission, in practice, deducts £1·10 per week, using its discretionary power to reduce benefit where there are exceptional circumstances.

The circumstances in which these deductions are to be made are that the claimant is required to register for work as a condition of receiving benefit (i.e. is classified as unemployed) and is disqualified from receiving unemployment benefit for one of the reasons set out in section 22(2) of the National Insurance Act, 1965, or would be so disqualified but for the fact that he has not claimed unemployment benefit or his claim has not yet been decided or has been disallowed on other grounds. The grounds for disqualification laid down in section 22(2) of the National Insurance Act are well summarized in paragraphs 19–21 of the leaflet on unemployment benefit (NI12, January 1970 edition) published by the Department of Health and Social Security:

Leaving a job voluntarily or being dismissed for misconduct

You may be disqualified from benefit for a period of up to six weeks if you leave your employment voluntarily without just cause or lose it through your misconduct.

Refusing to take a job offered

You may be disqualified from benefit for a period of up to six weeks if: –

(a) without good cause you have refused or failed to apply for, or refused to accept, suitable employment (see paragraph 21) notified to you by the Employment Exchange (or some other recognized agency or an employer or someone on behalf of an employer) as being vacant or about to become vacant, *or*

(b) you have failed to take a reasonable opportunity of employment, *or*

(c) without good cause you have refused or failed to carry out reasonable recommendations given to you in writing by an officer of the Employment Exchange to help you to find suitable employment, *or*

(d) without good cause you have refused or failed to avail yourself of a reasonable opportunity of receiving training, approved by the Department of Employment and Productivity in your case, for the purpose of securing regular employment.

Suitable employment

Suitable employment is normally employment in your usual occupation. But after a reasonable time, other employment may be regarded as suitable, if it is at a rate of wage not lower and on conditions not less favourable than those generally observed by agreement between associations of employers and of employees, or, failing any such agreement, than those generally recognized by good employers.

An offer of employment would not be regarded as suitable if, for example, it was: –

(a) employment in a situation vacant because of a stoppage of work due to a trade dispute, *or*

(b) employment in your usual occupation in the district where you were last ordinarily employed, at a rate of wage lower, or on conditions less favourable, than those which you might reasonably have expected to obtain there, *or*

(c) employment in your usual occupation in any other district at a rate of wage lower, or on conditions less favourable, than those generally observed or recognized in that district.

Decisions regarding entitlement to unemployment benefit are made by the insurance officer, subject to the claimant's right of appeal to the national insurance tribunal and to the National Insurance Commissioner. Once the insurance officer has ruled that the claimant is disqualified on one of the grounds mentioned above, the Commission must make the 40 per cent reduction, unless there are exceptional circumstances justifying a smaller reduction or payment of benefit in full. If the claimant appeals successfully against the disqualification, the deduction will be cancelled and arrears paid accordingly.

If no unemployment benefit claim has been made or the insurance officer has not yet made a decision or has disallowed the claim on other grounds, the responsibility for deciding whether there are grounds for disqualification under the National Insurance Act and, consequently, for applying the 40 per cent reduction falls on the Commission. Deductions of this sort made by the Commission should always be examined with great care, especially where no claim has been made for unemployment benefit, since the Commission's officers are not qualified, as the insurance officers are, to deal with the legal complexities of the National Insurance Act. A number of decisions by the National Insurance Commissioners, on such questions as the meaning of 'has voluntarily left such employment without just cause' or what is suitable employment, are to be found in the *Digest of Commissioners' Decisions*, which can be seen at the local national insurance office.

When the proposal to introduce the 40 per cent reduction, in place of the smaller discretionary reductions (usually 75p) imposed by the Commission in the past, was before Parliament, an assurance was given that the Commission would be asked to review its policy regarding the use of its discretionary powers in such cases, to ensure that hardship would not be caused. As a result of this review the Commission has instructed its officers to be on the alert for possible hardship, particularly in any of the following circumstances:

(a) Where there is sickness in the family or some unusual difficulty, however temporary;

(b) Where the rent has not been met in full because it is considered unreasonably high, or there are mortgage capital repayments or extensive hire-purchase commitments, and these outgoings cannot be met from disregarded income or capital;

(c) Where the claimant's last employment was of short duration;

(d) Where his last earnings were low in relation to his commitments;

(e) Where his wife is pregnant or there are very young children in the family.

If these instructions are complied with, the 40 per cent reduction should be waived in a considerable number of cases, especially where the claimant has a family to support. It is the Commission's policy, however, that where the full reduction would cause hardship there should still be a smaller reduction of benefit – at least 75p – so that disqualification from unemployment benefit should not be a matter of indifference to the claimant, as it might be if the Commission raised his income to the same level as if he were entitled to unemployment benefit.

The Commission recognizes the need to exercise discretion in this way only where hardship would result from the rigid application of the rule; but it can reasonably be asked to do so also where, although technically disqualified from receiving benefit under the National Insurance Act, the claimant is not guilty of any culpable misconduct. Disqualification under the national insurance scheme is not intended as a punishment but merely as a recognition of the principle underlying the scheme, that a man can only be insured against events for which he is not personally responsible. If he voluntarily chooses to remain out of work, he may have excellent reasons for doing so but there would be obvious objections to allowing him to continue drawing insurance benefit, which must be based on clear rules of entitlement and cannot take into account the full circumstances of each case. The Supplementary Benefits Commission can take such facts into account and should be asked to exercise its discretion in favour of claimants who would be unfairly penalized by the 40 per cent deduction, even where no hardship would be caused.

Refusal of benefit

Nowhere in either the Ministry of Social Security Act, 1966, or the Social Security Act, 1971, is there any mention of the possibility of supplementary benefit being refused or withdrawn on the grounds that the claimant is voluntarily un-employed. He can be offered a place at a re-establishment centre or required to attend a training course as a condition of receiving benefit (but only under a direction by the appeal tribunal and not if he is drawing unemployment insurance benefit), or his supplementary benefit can be reduced under the 1971 Act, but none of these actions is as extreme as that of cutting off his benefit altogether. The Commission, however, has a general power to reduce or withhold benefit as may be appropriate where there are exceptional circumstances, under paragraph 4(1) (b) of schedule 2 of the Ministry of Social Security Act. By using this discretionary power, the Commission can refuse or withdraw benefit without first applying to the appeal tribunal, and whether the claimant is in receipt of unemployment benefit or not.

It is, to say the least, questionable whether the Commission can properly treat as 'exceptional', for the purposes of paragraph 4(1) (b) of schedule 2, a situation for which specific provision is made elsewhere in the Act. By doing so, it deprives the claimant of the safeguards enacted by Parliament and at the same time imposes a more severe penalty than that to which those safeguards apply. It seems possible that this practice may be open to challenge on legal grounds (this would probably involve an appeal to the local tribunal followed by an application to the Divisional Court; see page 217). For the present, however, rightly or wrongly, the Commission regularly uses its discretionary powers in this way.

If a claimant is thought to be deliberately falling back on public funds when suitable work is available to him, supplementary benefit may simply be refused or cut off without prior notice. The *Handbook* mentions two types of case in which this happens. The first is where the claimant has committed one of the offences which would normally result in a reduction of his supplementary allowance under the 1971 Act (see pages 135–6) and 'it is known that there is a particular job, open to the claimant and suitable for him'. The second is where jobs are abundant in the area and the claimant is not a registered disabled person or seriously handicapped physically or mentally and has no dependants who would suffer hardship.

The Commission's concern (shared by most other people) that benefit should not be paid to persons for whom suitable work is available is entirely understandable. Nevertheless, there can be few cases in which outright refusal of benefit on such grounds does not involve some risk of both injustice and hardship. The Commission would no doubt argue that benefit is not refused unless there is convincing evidence that the claimant can support himself if compelled to do so, but one cannot feel happy about overworked officers, whose attitude to the unemployed (especially the young, long-haired unemployed) may not be entirely free of prejudice, being allowed to make instant decisions of this sort which may deprive a man of his only legitimate means of subsistence. The right of appeal offers little protection in these circumstances, since a month or more may elapse before the appeal is heard.

The 'four-week rule'

Before benefit can be refused or withdrawn under the Commission's discretionary powers, the officer making the decision must satisfy himself that there are exceptional circumstances in the particular case which justify this action. It cannot simply be assumed that a man is workshy; at the very least it must be shown that jobs are available which he could reasonably be expected to take. In effect, he must be presumed innocent until proved guilty. Under the procedure generally known as the four-week rule, however, an unemployed man is liable to have his benefit withdrawn after four weeks' notice, not because there is evidence that he is voluntarily unemployed, but because he has failed to produce evidence that he is *not* voluntarily unemployed. He is presumed guilty unless proved innocent.

The first thing to be said about the four-week rule is that it is not a rule at all but merely an administrative practice of very doubtful legality. It operates only in areas in which the Commission is advised by the Department of Employment that unskilled jobs can be obtained without difficulty, and affects only claimants under the age of 45 who (in the words of the *Handbook*) 'are free from any serious physical disability and ... have shown no signs of mental disorder or instability'. If the claimant is a single man and unskilled, he is told when he first claims benefit that payments will continue for up to four weeks, after which, if still unemployed, he will have to make a new claim. Married men, those with skills, and women are allowed to receive benefit for about three months while unemployed before a similar warning is issued to them.

Following complaints that claimants had not been advised of their right to reapply at the end of the four-week period, they now receive a printed form (form B663) at the beginning of the period, explaining the situation as follows:

SUPPLEMENTARY ALLOWANCE TO UNEMPLOYED CLAIMANT

Arrangements are being made with the Employment Exchange for payments to be made to you for a limited period while you look for a suitable job. In this area there are good openings for people under the age of 45 and we think you ought to be able to find work within the next four weeks.

You should look for work yourself as well as through the Employment Exchange, for example, by watching the advertisements in the local papers.

We hope you will find a suitable job without difficulty. If you experience any particular difficulty we should like to know about it.

If you are still unemployed at the end of four weeks, you can renew your claim for supplementary benefit, and you will then be specially interviewed. Unless there are good reasons why you cannot find suitable work, your allowance might be stopped at that time. If this were done you would be able to appeal against such a decision to an Appeal Tribunal.

It is important to note that the four-week warning, according to the Commission, is not a decision to refuse further benefit after four weeks. The only decision made at the beginning of the four weeks is the positive decision to pay benefit for up to four weeks. The decision to refuse further benefit is taken only if and when the claimant makes a further claim at the end of four weeks. The Commission, therefore, maintains that there is no right of appeal against the imposition of the four-week rule; the right of appeal arises only if the new claim is turned down. If a claimant attempts to lodge an appeal against the initial decision to limit his benefit to four weeks, the local social security office sees to it that the appeal does not reach the tribunal (in theory only the tribunal itself can decide whether an appeal is valid or not, but the Commission's officers frequently take it upon themselves to make such decisions). If the claimant reapplies for benefit at the end of the four weeks and is refused, he can then appeal, and payment of benefit will continue until the appeal hearing, though at a reduced rate – the reduction, although discretionary, is the same as that laid down by the Social Security Act, 1971, for 'disqualification' cases, 40 per cent of the scale rate for a single person.

There are strong grounds for arguing that the four-week rule is not only unjust but unlawful. If the Commission were to look into each case after four weeks, withdrawing benefit only if it found evidence that the claimant was not making reasonable efforts to find work, there would still be grounds for doubting whether this was a legitimate use of the discretionary power to withhold benefit where there are exceptional circumstances. Under the four-week rule, however, unless the claimant reapplies at the end of the four weeks, payment of benefit ceases without any attempt by the Commission to ascertain whether there are grounds for refusing further payments. It is true that the claimant has been told at the outset that he will be able to renew his claim if he is still unemployed, but the document quoted above, with its clear implication that failure to find work within four weeks will be regarded as evidence that he is workshy, together with the fact that a 'special' interview will follow, are likely to discourage him from making a further claim if he can possibly avoid doing so. If he does not renew his claim, the Commission is placed in the anomalous position of having withdrawn benefit without the slightest evidence of any change of circumstances or of the existence of exceptional circumstances which might justify such action. The Commission maintains that, since the claim has not been renewed, no decision has been made one way or the other as to whether the claimant is still entitled to benefit; all that has happened is that the original four weeks' award has expired. It is doubtful, however, whether the Commission can legally award benefit for a limited period in the absence of any evidence that entitlement will cease at the end of that period.

For practical purposes it makes little difference to the individual claimant whether the four-week rule, as at present administered, is legal or illegal. The important question is how to avoid having his benefit cut off. It is advisable, therefore, to submit a new claim at the end of the four-week period (using the ordinary claim form B1, obtained from the employment exchange), to attend for interview at the social security office when requested to do so, and if necessary to appeal against the refusal to continue payment of benefit. In the event of an appeal, the question to be decided by the tribunal will be whether the Commission was right to refuse benefit at the end of the four weeks, not whether it was right to issue the four-week warning in the first place. Nevertheless the tribunal should be reminded that it is in no way bound by the 'rule'. It may also help if the claimant can demonstrate (as he frequently can) that, whatever the rights and wrongs of the 'rule' itself, the way in which it was applied in his particular case was not in accordance with the procedure laid down by the Commission. Points to note in this connection include the following:

(a) The policy of the Commission is to operate the four-week rule only in areas where unskilled jobs are obtainable without difficulty. Evidence that such jobs are not readily available locally will therefore be helpful. (Such evidence should also be used to persuade the Commission, by representations at national level, that the area in question should be excluded from the operation of the rule. Representations are most likely to be effective if made to the Chairman of the Commission or the Secretary of State for Social Services by the local M.P. or a local body such as the trades council.)

(b) The rule does not apply to claimants aged 45 or over or who have a serious physical disability or have 'shown signs of mental disorder or instability'.

(c) Only in the case of single men who are unskilled is it the Commission's policy to issue the four-week warning when they first claim benefit. A number of cases have come to light in which this procedure was applied to men who were qualified for skilled work. This is particularly likely to happen if the man has said that he is prepared, if necessary, to take unskilled work rather than remain unemployed. It seems singularly unfair that, by thus demonstrating the genuineness of his wish to find work, he should render himself liable to have his benefit withdrawn after four weeks, when by insisting on a skilled job he could have continued to receive it for another three months.

(d) In some cases, benefit has been cut off after less than four weeks, or, where the Commission's policy is to issue the four-week warning only after benefit has been paid for three months, this period has not been allowed to elapse.

(e) Cases have been reported in which form B663, informing the claimant of the right to renew his claim and to appeal against a refusal to continue paying benefit, was not issued.

(f) Even if form B663 was issued, the claimant may have received incorrect information from officials, either at the employment exchange or at the social security office, regarding the operation of the rule and his rights in relation to it. This need not imply any intention to mislead: the Commission's tortuous reasoning on this question is not easily understood even by its own officers, still less by the staff of the Department of Employment, so it is not surprising if the explanations they give are sometimes inaccurate.

Above all, it should be remembered that an unemployed person who is in need of supplementary benefit, according to the standards laid down in the regulations, has both a moral and a legal right to receive such benefit, unless it can be shown that there are exceptional circumstances which justify withholding it. The onus is on the Commission to show that such circumstances exist; otherwise, there should be no question of benefit being either refused or withdrawn.

OTHER DISCRETIONARY DEDUCTIONS

In addition to the types of case mentioned above, other cases may occasionally occur in which the Commission uses its power to reduce or withhold benefit where there are exceptional circumstances (see, for example, pages 174 and 184). Such cases should always be examined very carefully to ensure both that there are genuinely exceptional circumstances and that the reduction or refusal or benefit can be considered 'appropriate to take account of those circumstances', as required by paragraph 4(1) of schedule 2 of the Ministry of Social Security Act.

Chapter 6

FAMILY RESPONSIBILITY

Anybody in Great Britain over the age of 16 can claim supplementary benefit, provided that he satisfies the conditions laid down in the Ministry of Social Security Act. Those under 16, though unable to claim in their own right, can be included in a claim as dependants. Similarly, a woman living with her husband cannot herself make a claim, but her needs will be taken into account in assessing the total requirements of her husband if he claims supplementary benefit. Thus the normal unit of assessment is the basic family unit of husband, wife and children, and the claim for benefit must be made by the husband. A single woman, widow or a separated or divorced wife, however, can claim in her own right for herself and any dependent children living with her, just as a single man can. On receiving such a claim, the Commission's first responsibility is to assess the claimant's entitlement to benefit in the light of her financial circumstances at the time. The fact that a woman may be separated or divorced or the mother of an illegitimate child does not affect her entitlement, but it may mean that her husband or ex-husband, or the father of her child, has a legal liability for maintaining her and/or her children. Section 22 of the Ministry of Social Security Act provides that, for the purposes of the Act, a man is liable to maintain his wife and children, including illegitimate children of whom he has been adjudged the father (in Scotland he becomes liable for an illegitimate child if he admits paternity or it is otherwise legally established); and a woman is liable to maintain her husband and her children, including illegitimate children. If either a man or a woman (in practice it is usually the man) fails to fulfil this legal liability, the Commission may be obliged to fill the gap by payment of supplementary benefit. If it does so, however, it will want to be sure that the failure is genuine and not a 'put-up job' to enable the woman to claim benefit. The Commission will also want to recover as much as possible of the money it has paid out from the 'liable relative', and to ensure that he (or she) does not default in future.

Liability to maintain, for the purposes of the Act, does not normally extend beyond the responsibility of husbands and wives for each other and that of parents for their children. In one respect, however, the Act goes further than this. Paragraph 3 of schedule 2 provides that, if a couple are 'cohabiting as man and wife', they (and their dependent children) are to be treated as a single unit for supplementary benefit purposes, just as if they were legally married, unless there are exceptional circumstances. As a result, the woman loses her right to claim benefit independently for herself and her children, although the man is legally liable only for the maintenance of his own children, not for the woman or any children she has had by another man.

These provisions of the Act and the circumstances which bring them into operation in particular cases are a constant source of difficulties both for claimants and for the Commission. In this chapter, therefore, their practical implications and the way in which they are administered by the Commission will be considered in detail.

SEPARATED WIVES

If a woman claims supplementary benefit as the result of separation from her husband (whether he has left her or she him), her requirements and those of her children who are living with her are assessed in the normal way. In calculating the resources to be set against the family's requirements to arrive at the amount of benefit payable, the husband's resources are ignored, only the amount he is actually paying to the wife being taken into account. At the beginning of a separation, the allowance may have to be reassessed from week to week until the situation has been stabilized.

A separated wife applying for benefit for the first time may be questioned in some detail about the circumstances of her separation. Such inquiries may be necessary to enable the Commission to decide what action, if any, should be taken to induce the husband to fulfil his obligations. Moreover, cases of 'collusive desertion' are known to occur, in which the wife denies knowledge of her husband's whereabouts although he is in fact either still living with her or has temporarily moved out so that she can claim benefit. The Commission obviously has a duty to guard against this possibility and it is by no means easy to distinguish between cases where the separation has been arranged in order to obtain supplementary benefit and those in which there are other causes of the separation, especially as even in the latter case the man's decision to leave may have been influenced by the knowledge that his wife would be supported by the Commission.

If the husband's whereabouts can be established, he is contacted by an officer of the Commission to ascertain his proposals for meeting his responsibility to maintain his wife and children, to the extent that he is able to do so. If his income is very low or he has other commitments (e.g. he may be living with another woman and supporting his illegitimate children), it may not be realistic to expect him to make payments to his wife of an amount that will remove her need to claim supplementary benefit. In that event, the Commission may agree to his paying such amounts as he can afford, subject to periodic review of his circumstances to see whether the payments can be increased. If the husband is himself drawing supplementary benefit, he will probably be unable to pay anything to his wife, since his benefit will be calculated on the basis of his own requirements and those of any dependants living with him. The requirements of his dependants who are not members of his household are not taken into account in assessing his needs, even though he is legally obliged to maintain them. It would theoretically be possible for the

Commission to increase his benefit on grounds of exceptional circumstances to enable him to meet his obligations to his wife and children, but in practice this is not done.

Provided that the husband agrees to make what the Commission regards as reasonable payments towards the support of his family, and fulfils his undertaking regularly, the wife should receive supplementary benefit to meet the balance of her weekly requirements without further difficulty, subject to the normal conditions (e.g. if she has no children under 16 she may have to register for work as a condition of receiving benefit). Complications arise where the husband refuses or fails to make reasonable provision for his dependants when able to do so. In this situation, several courses of action are available to the Commission:

(a) The wife can be encouraged to apply to the Magistrates' Court for a maintenance order, but she is not obliged to do so, and her right to supplementary benefit will not be affected if she refuses.

(b) If the wife is unable or unwilling to apply for a maintenance order, the Commission may do so under section 23 of the Ministry of Social Security Act. (There is a six months' time-limit for a complaint to the Magistrates' Court by the wife, but applications by the Commission under section 23 are not subject to this limit.)

(c) If civil proceedings are ineffective, or cannot be taken because the man's whereabouts are unknown, the Commission may take criminal proceedings, under section 30, against a man who persistently refuses or neglects to maintain himself or any person whom, for the purposes of the Act, he is liable to maintain and whose needs therefore have to be met by the Commission. For this purpose, the Commission may apply for a warrant for the man's arrest. On conviction he is liable to imprisonment for up to three months and/or a fine of up to £100.

If the Commission applies to the Court for a maintenance order, it will normally be limited to the amount of benefit in payment to the wife and will lapse if for any reason her benefit ceases (because, for example, she decides to go out to work). The Commission's policy is therefore to encourage the wife to make her own application. The Court may then order payments of a larger amount than the rate of benefit she is receiving, the order will remain in force if she ceases to receive benefit, and (in the words of the *Handbook*) 'the possibility of reconciliation will receive proper consideration when she is brought into direct contact with the Court officials'.

The fact that a Court order has been made is of course no guarantee that it will be complied with; in fact most Court orders in favour of separated wives receiving supplementary benefit are complied with only partially, if that. When the husband fails to pay, the wife's benefit for the particular week is increased accordingly, so that she is no worse off. She may, however, suffer a good deal of inconvenience in the process. To prevent this and to give the woman the security of knowing that she will get a regular income whether her husband complies with the Court order or not, the Magistrates' Clerk will usually allow her to authorize payment to the Department of Health and Social Security of any money received from the husband under the order. The Commission will then be able to issue an order-book at the full rate of her supplementary benefit entitlement, without regard to the payments received from her husband. The woman is free to cancel the authority at any time and revert to receiving the money direct from the Clerk's office. In Scotland, the procedure is different because payments under a maintenance order are not made through the Court; but it may be possible to make a similar arrangement under which the Department collects the money direct from the husband or from the woman's solicitor if payments are made to him.

This method of relieving the woman of the anxiety and uncertainty of relying on maintenance payments, which may arrive late or not at all, generally works well and is a great help to separated wives. But it can only be used with the agreement of the social security office. If the woman's income, including the payments due under the Court order, is below supplementary benefit level and likely to remain so for some time to come, there will seldom be any objection; indeed, the Commission's officers normally take the initiative in suggesting that the order should be 'signed over'. The situation is more complicated where the payments under the Court order are sufficient to raise the woman's income up to or above supplementary benefit level and the need for benefit only arises when the husband fails to pay up. If the order is signed over to the DHSS, and the husband then makes regular payments of the full amount ordered by the Court, there will be an additional sum due to the wife each week over and above her normal supplementary benefit. From the point of view of the Commission, this involves the extra work of calculating the underpayment and sending it to the woman; while for her it means some delay in receiving part of her weekly income. The Commission is therefore reluctant to suggest or agree to such an arrangement unless it is clear that the husband is unlikely to comply with the order regularly.

A husband who is thinking of returning to his wife may be worried about the possibility of his being asked to repay the supplementary benefit she has received in his absence. The *Handbook*, in fact, warns that this may happen. The Commission, however, cannot *require* him to make such a repayment without first obtaining a Court order under section 23 of the Act; and in making an order the Magistrates must have regard to his financial situation at the time when his wife was receiving benefit, ignoring any improvement that may have taken place since then. In practice, it is not likely that the Commission would go to the length of taking a man to Court if it was clear that he intended to support his family in future, unless his current resources were well above the family's requirements by supplementary benefit standards.

DIVORCED WOMEN

Once a couple are divorced, their liability to maintain each other under section 22 of the Ministry of Social Security Act comes to an end, though there may well be a Court order or voluntary agreement regarding the woman's maintenance. Each of them remains liable under section 22 for the support of the children but, again, the division of responsibility between them will usually be the subject of a Court order or agreement. The question of 'collusive desertion' will not arise, so the woman should have no difficulty in obtaining supplementary benefit if she is eligible for it, once the legal position has been made clear.

A Court order in favour of a divorced woman or her children can be 'signed over' to the Department of Health and Social Security in the same way as that of a separated wife. Before doing this, however, it will be necessary to have the order registered in the Magistrates' Court – a simple procedure on which the Magistrates' Clerk will advise. As with separated wives, different arrangements have to be made in Scotland.

UNMARRIED MOTHERS

As in the case of a separated wife, the Commission has a duty to ensure that an unmarried mother who is eligible to claim benefit (i.e. over 16, not in full-time work, etc.) has an income sufficient to meet her requirements and those of her child or children, and that all reasonable steps are taken to persuade the father of an illegitimate child to pay for its maintenance to the extent that he is able to do so. He is not legally liable for the maintenance of the mother, but the amount he is asked (or ordered by the Court) to contribute towards the child's maintenance may well exceed the amount of benefit payable in respect of the child, in which case the balance of his contributions will serve to reduce the amount of benefit needed by the mother in order to meet her own requirements.

The methods of persuasion available are much the same as in the case of an absent husband. The mother can apply for an affiliation order, normally within twelve months of the birth of the child in England and Wales. If she is unwilling or the time limit has expired the application can be made by the Commission under section 24 of the Ministry of Social Security Act. Once the Court has made an order, if the father still fails to pay, he can be prosecuted under section 30 of the Act. The mother is encouraged to apply for the affiliation order herself, so that the maintenance payments will continue if she ceases to draw supplementary benefit; and she is normally allowed to sign over the payments to the DHSS in the same way as a separated wife.

Many unmarried mothers are unwilling either to take the father of their child to Court or to disclose his identity so that the Commission can do so. There are many possible reasons for this reluctance, ranging from the mother's wish to remain independent of the man to her fear that taking him to Court may destroy her chances of marrying him. Whatever the reason, she has a perfect right to refuse to co-operate in this way, and her refusal does not affect her right to supplementary benefit. The Commission, however, while fully recognizing this, must do all it reasonably can to identify the father, in order to ensure that he meets his legal responsibility for the maintenance of his child. The Commission's officers are therefore required to discuss the child's paternity with the mother, but their instructions are that, if after due reflection she remains unwilling to name the father, the matter is not to be pursued. Under no circumstances should a mother be persuaded against her will to name the child's father, or threatened with the withdrawal of benefit if she fails to do so. It is important that mothers in this situation should be aware that, while it may well be in their own interests that the father should be taken to Court, they are not obliged to name him if they do not want to.

There are no exceptions to the rule that a person under 16 cannot claim supplementary benefit. A girl under 16 who has a baby is therefore not eligible for benefit in her own right, though she can claim free welfare milk and foods on grounds of low income. If she is living with either or both of her parents who are themselves receiving or claiming supplementary benefit or a family income supplement, both the girl and her baby can be counted as their dependants in assessing their entitlement to either of these benefits. They will also normally be able to claim a family allowance and income-tax allowance for the baby if it is being maintained by them.

COHABITATION

The Ministry of Social Security Act provides, in paragraph 3(1) of schedule 2, that the requirements and resources of a couple who are 'cohabiting as man and wife' but are not married to each other are to be aggregated in the same way as those of a married couple, unless there are exceptional circumstances. Thus the woman cannot claim or continue to receive benefit in her own right but is treated as a dependant of the man. The assumption underlying this rule is that the needs of a man and woman who are living together as if they were married are no different from those of a couple who have actually gone through a marriage ceremony, and that it would therefore be unfair to treat them differently. If there were no cohabitation rule, there would in some cases be a financial advantage in remaining unmarried, and this might be regarded as an encouragement to immorality. The Commission's views on the cohabitation rule and a description of the way in which it is administered are to be found in a report by the Commission, *Cohabitation: the administration of the relevant provisions of the Ministry of Social Security Act 1966*, published in 1971.

There are, of course, many cases in which two people are living as a married couple although not legally married, are known to those around them as Mr and Mrs —, and would not wish to be treated differently from a legally married couple. Indeed, the Commission might possibly pay benefit to the man in respect of his 'wife's' needs without being aware of the true situation. In cases of this kind, the cohabitation rule poses no difficulty. But the facts are not always so simple and, as the *Cohabitation* report says, 'even when the facts are known and admitted, the decision on whether or not cohabitation exists is, in the last resort, a matter of personal judgement'. It is, however, a matter on which some general guide lines have been laid down in cases decided by the Courts in other connections. The *Handbook* provides a useful summary of the factors which have to be considered:

There is no simple answer. The decision has to be reached after weighing up a combination of facts, e.g. Is there a common home? Is there a pooled household fund? Do the couple have children? What are the regular sleeping arrangements? Does the woman use the man's name and are the couple acknowledged publicly as man and wife? And so on.

The answer to any one question is not necessarily conclusive by itself. Nor need the answer to any one question be more significant, taken by itself, than the answer to another. In each case all the facts have to be regarded as a whole in reaching a decision. And it should be emphasised that the decision depends solely on whether it appears that the couple are living as man and wife in the full sense of the term, not on any moral considerations or on whether a man and woman have slept together on occasions.

There is a further distinction to be made between cases where the relationship between the two people concerned, whether constituting cohabitation or not, is a stable one, and cases where the situation is changing. In the latter case, the Commission has to decide at precisely what stage in the relationship the supplementary benefit in payment to one or both of the parties should be recalculated or withdrawn on the grounds that they are now cohabiting. In the absence of an exact definition, it is extremely difficult to know when that stage has been reached; and it is still more difficult for the Commission to obtain the information on which such a decision must be based, especially as the couple will have a direct interest in maintaining that they are living as two single persons (the benefit payable on that basis will nearly always be more than they would be entitled to as a married or cohabiting couple). The type of case where this difficulty arises most frequently is that of a woman with children who is in receipt of a supplementary allowance and is suspected of cohabiting with a man who is in full-time work. If they are treated as if they were living as man and wife, and there are no exceptional circumstances, the woman will no longer be able to claim benefit in her own right. Her needs and those of the children could be added to those of the man if he were himself in a position to claim – but he is not, since he is in full-time work (if his earnings are low, they may be able to make a joint claim for family income supplement; see pages 187–97). Thus the whole of the benefit previously drawn by the woman is withdrawn and she becomes, at one stroke, partially if not wholly dependent on the man for the maintenance of herself and her children. At best, the Commission may agree to continue paying benefit to meet the needs of the children, usually only for a short period (see page 159).

In view of the difficulties inherent in the administration of the cohabitation rule, it is not surprising that the Commission sometimes resorts to some fairly unsavoury methods of obtaining evidence of cohabitation. As the *Cohabitation* report explains, inquiries may be set off by 'an anonymous letter which may be spiteful and unfounded' and the Commission's 'special investigators' (officers specially trained to uncover cases of fraud) 'may have to make local enquiries without the knowledge of the claimant or to watch a house to see who lives there. This is distasteful work, to the investigator as well as to the claimant and others concerned. But it is the price that has to be paid for administering the cohabitation rule.' The report says nothing about the damage such investigations may do to the reputation of the victims of 'spiteful and unfounded' allegations. It admits, however, that the evidence on the basis of which a woman may lose her sole source of income may be far from conclusive:

Critics of the system sometimes complain that evidence obtained in this way is acted upon though it would not stand up in a court of law. This shows a fundamental misunderstanding of the object of special enquiries in cases of suspected cohabitation. They are not intended to be automatically a preliminary to a prosecution, for which, in any case, the evidence must be such as to establish guilt beyond all reasonable doubt. They are intended to discover facts on which to make a judgment about the case as a whole. This will include a decision as to whether, on the balance of probabilities, cohabitation is shown – a judgment which can be challenged forthwith in an informal appeal tribunal.

It is, unfortunately, by no means the case that the decision to cut off a woman's benefit can be 'challenged forthwith', since it may be a month or more before her appeal is heard by the tribunal. Moreover, the tribunal will also make its decision 'on the balance of probabilities' and, although theoretically independent, may well be influenced by the fact that the Commission considered the evidence strong enough to justify withdrawal of benefit.

Despite the complacent tone of the *Cohabitation* report as a whole, it announced some minor safeguards against the cutting off of benefit on the basis of inadequate evidence. First, the Commission's officers had been instructed that, if a couple suspected of cohabiting had not publicly acknowledged that they were living as man and wife (e.g. by using the same surname on the electoral register, or by 'a previous claim of any kind by the man in which he recognised the woman as a dependant'), no further inquiries were to be made without the authority of a senior officer; and such authority was to be given only where there was 'some actual evidence justifying further investigations', such as 'the birth of a child of the union; information that the couple are known as a married couple in the neighbourhood; indications, for example, from their going on holidays together, that their relationship might be other than the usual landlady/lodger one; or the obvious unsuitability of the accommodation for a lodger'.

The second change in the instructions to officers, also announced in the report, was that 'considerable emphasis should be placed on the stability of a union as evidence of cohabitation and that, conversely, the fact that a woman receives an occasional visitor, whether he sleeps with her or not, does not of itself justify a decision that there is cohabitation'. The fact that such an instruction was necessary is an indication of the loose way in which the cohabitation rule was interpreted in the past. Especially revealing is the Commission's comment that 'adherence to this instruction will frequently lead to criticism, especially in the case of a woman who has a number of men visitors who stay overnight or a woman who receives frequent visits from the same man'. It is possible that frequent visits from the same man might be evidence of cohabitation (though a visiting relationship is hardly what most people would regard as living as man and wife); but the fact that a woman has a number of men visitors who stay overnight, whatever else it indicates, certainly does not suggest that she and any one of her visitors are living as man and wife.

Any woman who feels that her benefit has been wrongfully withdrawn on the grounds that she is cohabiting with a man should of course appeal to the local tribunal without delay. It is important to remember, moreover, that the question of what constitutes cohabitation is a very complicated one. Even if the couple are inclined to accept that the Commission's interpretation of the situation may be legally correct, it is always worth while to seek skilled advice on this question. Some possible sources of such advice are suggested in Chapter 9. See pages 207–8.

Cohabitation and 'exceptional circumstances'

Although the fact that two people are cohabiting as man and wife normally means that their requirements and resources must be aggregated for supplementary benefit purposes and that the woman can no longer claim in her own right, paragraph 3(1) of schedule 2 of the Ministry of Social Security Act qualifies the cohabitation rule with the magic words 'unless there are exceptional circumstances'. Thus, if it can be shown that there are exceptional circumstances in a particular case, the Commission may treat the couple as two single individuals, even if they are openly cohabiting as man and wife. As usual, it is left to the Commission (or the appeal tribunal) to decide what circumstances should be regarded as exceptional.

In practice, there is only one type of case in which the Commission is likely to concede that there are circumstances justifying payment of benefit to a woman who is cohabiting, and that is where the woman has a child or children of a former union. Since the man with whom she is now living is not the children's father, he is not legally liable for their maintenance, although the cohabitation rule assumes implicitly that he will in fact maintain them. On 2 May 1972, Sir Keith Joseph, Secretary of State for Social Services, announced an important relaxation of the cohabitation rule in relation to cases of this kind:

The Commission have decided that in these circumstances they will use their discretionary powers to continue to pay supplementary benefit where necessary to meet those children's requirements for a period of 4 weeks to give the family time to adapt to the changed circumstances. After that time some benefit will continue to be paid if the resources of the whole family (including the man's earnings and Family Income Supplement) are insufficient for their requirements – that is, are below supplementary benefit level.

What this means is that, instead of the woman's benefit being cut off immediately, it will continue for four weeks at a reduced rate, arrived at by taking the supplementary benefit scale rates for the children and deducting any other income available to meet their needs, such as family allowances and any payments made by their own father. At the end of this period, if the couple are still cohabiting and the man is in full-time work, benefit will continue only to the extent necessary to raise their combined resources to supplementary benefit level. If his earnings are sufficient to achieve this aim, no further payments will be made. Any payments he has to make for the maintenance of his legal wife and/or children will be allowed as a deduction from his income in deciding whether benefit should continue.

Despite this small concession, the Commission's policy with regard to the payment of benefit in exceptional circumstances to women who are cohabiting remains, in general, extremely rigid. The Commission argues, in the *Handbook*, that by definition exceptional circumstances must be rare. Yet in many other connections the Commission takes a much broader view of what is an exceptional circumstance (for example, when paying extra allowances to old people for heating, domestic help, laundry, etc.). There are undoubtedly many cases of cohabitation in which the woman's benefit need not be cut off if the Commission were willing to adopt an equally liberal interpretation of 'exceptional circumstances' in this context.

Unfortunately, the appeal tribunals tend to be as reluctant as the Commission itself to use their discretionary powers in the claimant's favour in cases where cohabitation is alleged. Nevertheless, if it can be argued that hardship is being caused by the withdrawal of benefit and that there are exceptional circumstances which would enable the tribunal to reverse the Commission's decision, it may be worth lodging an appeal. It may also be helpful, where a woman is appealing against the decision that she is cohabiting, to point out to the tribunal that, even if they decide that the couple are living as man and wife, it may still be possible to reinstate her benefit under the exceptional circumstances provision.

If the Commission has already agreed to continue paying benefit in respect of the children's requirements for four weeks, under the new policy described above, it will usually be worth appealing both against the restriction of the amount of benefit and against its withdrawal at the end of the four weeks. The fact that payment of benefit has continued at all implies that the Commission has accepted that there are exceptional circumstances. Since both the decision to pay benefit only for the children and the decision to withdraw it after four weeks are discretionary, there is always a possibility that the appeal tribunal may be disposed to make more generous use of its discretionary powers.

Chapter 7

SOME SPECIAL CASES

In this chapter we shall consider a number of cases which are, in one way or another, out of the ordinary and to which, therefore, special rules or policies apply: hospital patients, people living in old people's homes and other residential institutions, students, and people going or coming from abroad.

HOSPITAL PATIENTS

The Ministry of Social Security Act provides, in paragraph 16 of schedule 2, for the requirements of a 'person residing as patient in any hospital' to be assessed at 'such amount, if any, as may be appropriate, having regard to all the circumstances'. The amount of benefit paid to a hospital patient is thus left to the judgement of the Commission, subject to the usual right of appeal. The rules laid down by the Commission as a guide to its officers in dealing with the varying circumstances of patients and their families are described in the *Handbook*, which explains that 'the Commission's general aim is to ensure that the hospital inpatient has sufficient resources to cover any continuing commitments such as home rent or the requirements of his dependants, with a margin for his own personal expenses while in hospital'. The details given below are based mainly on the relevant sections of the *Handbook*.

Married patients

If a husband or wife is admitted to hospital for a short time, payment of supplementary benefit continues at the same rate as if they were both still living at home, except that a discretionary addition, e.g. for a special diet, may be discontinued if the need for which it was intended is now being met by the hospital. The Commission assumes that any financial saving to the family through having one less mouth to feed will be roughly balanced by the cost of visiting the patient and other incidental expenses.

After eight weeks, if the patient is still in hospital, the couple's requirements are reduced by £1·35 a week, but special consideration is given to the question of fares for visiting and, if necessary, help is given either by a discretionary addition to the weekly benefit payment or, if frequent visits are not required, by exceptional needs payments. The £1·35 reduction is the same as the reduction of national insurance benefits after eight weeks in hospital. If the patient is drawing sickness or other insurance benefit as well as supplementary benefit, therefore, what usually happens is that the insurance benefit is reduced and the supplementary benefit remains the same. If supplementary benefit alone is in payment, it will be reduced. In either case the couple's income goes down by £1·35. The eight-week period need not be continuous; if the patient is discharged and readmitted within twenty-eight days, the two periods in hospital are added together for this purpose, and if benefit had been reduced in the first period the reduction will apply immediately on readmission.

Apart from this £1·35 reduction, the couple's supplementary benefit is not affected by the absence of one of them in hospital unless he or she remains there for more than two years and there is then no prospect of fairly early discharge. At that stage the patient will no longer be regarded as a member of the joint household and will be treated in the same way as a single person without dependants (see below). The requirements of the partner left at home will be assessed separately, due allowance being made for the cost of visiting the patient.

The assumption that the couple's needs remain unchanged for the first eight weeks and then fall by £1·35 per week is administratively convenient and avoids the need for minor adjustments at a time when both husband and wife are preoccupied with other anxieties. It is, however, always possible to ask for an increase in benefit if the expenses resulting from the patient's admission to hospital are greater than the corresponding savings.

Single patients

If the patient is a single person (including a separated or divorced husband or wife or a widow or widower), they will be assumed to need £1·35 per week for personal expenses (£1·60 for a person suffering from respiratory tuberculosis) plus an allowance for any outside commitments. These will normally include rent, rates and a standing charge for gas and electricity. They may also include hire-purchase instalments which have to be kept up. If the stay in hospital is prolonged, however, the Commission may not be prepared to continue paying for such outside commitments. If the patient has a home of his own, the rent and other outgoings will normally be met for the first three months, after which, the *Handbook* warns, 'if it appears that no foreseeable date can be set for his discharge from hospital, the question will have to be considered how much longer an allowance should be paid in respect of these items'. After three months it will usually be clear whether the patient is likely to be able to return to his own home at some stage or not. So long as the possibility exists, the Commission should be prepared to continue making any necessary payments to keep the home available. Even where the medical evidence suggests that the patient will never return home, it may still be justifiable to continue meeting the rent for a few months longer, if only on humanitarian grounds. Nevertheless, there will inevitably be some cases where it would be indefensible to do so indefinitely. Precisely where to draw the line can only be decided in the light of the circumstances in each case. It is worth noting that, where necessary, the local authority can arrange and pay for the storage of furniture if a patient is compelled to give up his home.

In the case of a single person who, before entering hospital, was living as a boarder in a private household or as a resident in a home or hostel run by a voluntary body, the Commission will enable him to pay a 'reasonable' retaining fee for the accommodation for the first eight weeks in hospital, or longer 'where special considerations justify it'. The loss of accommodation of this kind may not seem such a serious matter as expecting a person to give up his own home, but the psychological implications may not be very different and the allowance towards the retaining fee should not be cut off so long as there is a reasonable prospect of the patient returning to the accommodation within another month or two.

If a single person with children has to be admitted to hospital, the amount of benefit payable will depend on the arrangements made for the care of the children. Benefit will not be paid to meet the needs of the children if they are taken into the care of the local authority, but if the parent has to pay for them to be cared for in some other way an allowance can be paid for this purpose, the amount of which will depend on the circumstances. The local authority social services department, which has an interest in seeing that satisfactory arrangements are made for the children, since they may otherwise have to be taken into its care, may be prepared to assist with the costs involved if the allowance made by the Commission is not sufficient.

Children in hospital

If a child whose parents are entitled to supplementary benefit is admitted to hospital, their benefit remains unaltered for the first twelve weeks; it is assumed that the savings resulting from the child's absence from home will be balanced by the extra expenses of visiting etc. If the expenses are more than the savings, an additional allowance can be requested, in the same way as for an adult in hospital. (See pages 163–4.) After twelve weeks, instead of the normal scale rate for the child, only 75p a week is allowed, unless there are circumstances (including the cost of visiting the child) which justify a higher allowance. This may seem unfair, since the family may still be drawing both family allowance and a national insurance dependency allowance in respect of the child in hospital, amounting to £2·10 or in some cases more. By allowing only 75p, the Commission is in effect saying that part of these allowances should be used to meet the needs of other members of the family than the child on whose account they are payable. The Commission, however, is concerned only with the family's total income and whether it is sufficient to meet its requirements. The allowance of 75p a week will only be increased, therefore, if it can be shown to be insufficient in the circumstances of the particular case. The mere fact that more than this is being spent on visiting the child and on toys, sweets and other expenses for the child's benefit will not necessarily convince the Commission that an increase is justified, since it may not regard the whole of the expenditure as necessary. If a disagreement arises on this point, it may be worth appealing to the tribunal.

Mental patients

Arrangements regarding patients in hospitals for the mentally ill and the mentally sub-normal are similar to those described above for other hospital patients, except that the responsibility for providing them with pocket money at present rests with the Hospital Management Committee. The allowance of £1·35 which the Commission normally makes for the personal expenses of a single claimant in hospital does not apply, therefore, to mental patients (other than those in general hospitals), who have to rely on the discretion of the hospital authorities for their spending money. The maximum payment is £1·35, but this may be reduced if the doctor responsible for the patient considers that, because of his medical condition, the full amount cannot be used for his personal comfort or enjoyment. This distinction between mental and other patients has been criticized as undignified, unnecessary and a possible source of injustice, and the Commission has agreed in principle to take over the payment of pocket money to mental patients – but not until the necessary additional manpower and money are made available.

Apart from mental patients, there are cases in which the medical officer responsible for the treatment of a hospital patient considers that the normal allowance for personal expenses cannot be used for the patient's personal comfort and enjoyment, for example because of advanced senility. If the patient has been in hospital for a year or more, his benefit is reduced accordingly or withdrawn altogether. This is in keeping with the national insurance regulations which provide for a similar reduction of national insurance benefits in such cases.

Patients on leave

Hospital patients sent home, or to stay with relatives or friends, for weekends or other short periods, whether as part of their treatment or to meet the hospital's convenience, are entitled to supplementary benefit at the full rate for each complete day spent away from the hospital.

OLD PEOPLE'S HOMES IN ENGLAND AND WALES

The responsibility for providing accommodation for 'persons who by reason of age, infirmity or any other circumstances are in need of care and attention which is not otherwise available to them' is placed on local authorities in England and Wales by section 21 of part III of the National Assistance Act, 1948; hence it is generally known as 'part III accommodation'. It can be provided either directly by the local authority or by arrangement with voluntary bodies. Some local authorities have special schemes under the Health Services and Public Health Act, 1968, enabling them to make similar arrangements with private persons. If the local authority makes use of voluntary or private old people's homes in this way, it accepts financial responsibility for the cost of maintaining old people placed in them. This responsibility, however, extends only to old people in need of care and attention not otherwise available. If an old person goes to live in a voluntary or private home as a matter of convenience rather than of necessity, he is in much the same position as if he were a lodger in a private household, and the local authority has no responsibility for his maintenance. Moreover, even if the local authority accepts responsibility under part III, and has made financial arrangements with a particular home, it may not be willing to maintain an old person in that home if it has room in its own homes.

These arrangements have a direct effect on the amount of supplementary benefit payable. Paragraph 15 of schedule 2 of the Ministry of Social Security Act provides that the requirements of a person in *part III accommodation* are to be assessed at the amounts prescribed by the Secretary of State as the minimum rate of payment for accommodation and personal requirements. The amounts prescribed for a single person in part III accommodation are at present £5·40 for accommodation and £1·35 for personal requirements, making a total of £6·75 a week. As this is also the standard retirement pension rate under the national insurance scheme, it follows that an old person living in part III accommodation and in receipt of a retirement pension will not normally be eligible for a supplementary pension. This applies whether the accommodation is provided directly by the local authority or by arrangement with a voluntary body or private persons. The charge for accommodation in a voluntary or private home is usually far more than £5·40 a week, but the difference must be met by the local authority if it has accepted financial responsibility for the person concerned.

If an old person moves to, or is already living in, a *private or voluntary home* and the local authority has not accepted financial responsibility for his maintenance, his requirements are assessed under paragraph 17 of schedule 2 (dealing with persons paying an inclusive charge for board and lodging) at 'such amount as may be appropriate' but not less than the 'non-householder' rate of £5·80 for a supplementary pensioner under 80, or £6·05 for those over 80. In the case of a voluntary home, or a private home where the local authority has a special scheme, if, in principle, the local authority could accept responsibility (i.e. the old person is in need of care and attention not otherwise available to him), the Commission assesses the requirements at £6·75 a week – the 'part III' rate – and leaves the management of the home to persuade the local authority to accept responsibility for the balance of the weekly charge. If the local authority refuses, the Commission should be asked to reconsider its decision, and, depending on the reason given for the refusal, it may be prepared to allow a higher amount. In other cases, where the local authority has no power to accept financial responsibility, the Commission follows its normal practice for dealing with boarders, taking the weekly requirements to be the board and lodging charge, or as much of it as is reasonable, plus an allowance of £2·10 for personal expenses. In deciding what is a reasonable board and lodging charge for this purpose, the Commission recognizes that a higher charge may be justified than would be normal for younger persons and is therefore prepared to meet in full a charge which is up to £2 a week higher than would normally be regarded as reasonable for board and lodging in the neighbourhood. If the charge is still higher, as will often be the case, and the Commission cannot be persuaded to meet it in full, there are several possible solutions. The claimant may be able to meet part of the weekly charge out of savings, or a charitable body or relatives may be prepared to assist (if so, the Commission will generally disregard any such assistance, under its discretionary powers, if either the old person's capital does not exceed £800 or the fees are not considered excessively high). In the case of a private home, if the local authority has a special scheme but has not exercised its powers to make financial arrangements with the home under part III of the National Assistance Act, it may be willing to consider doing so. And if other solutions fail, the claimant can appeal to the local tribunal against the Commission's decision. Only as a last resort should he be expected to move to cheaper accommodation or to a local authority home.

From the point of view of the old person's financial situation, the main difference between the treatment of 'part III' and 'board and lodging' cases often lies in the allowance made for personal expenses – £1·35 in one case and £2·10 in the other. The *Handbook* explains this difference on the grounds that those in private homes 'usually have to meet the cost of such items as clothing, toilet requisites, etc.', for which the local authority is responsible in part III accommodation. There may, however, be grounds for asking for the higher allowance to be made where an old person in a voluntary home is assessed on the 'part III' basis but is not in fact being supported by the local authority.

It is important that the financial arrangements and possible future difficulties should be clarified *before* an old person moves into a voluntary or private home. Difficulties are sometimes caused by failure to approach the local authority until the old person has already been admitted to the home. Similarly, if it is likely that, at any stage, the Commission will be asked to help with the fees for a private home, it is advisable to ascertain at the outset what proportion it will be prepared to meet. It is also important to bear in mind that the old person can claim supplementary benefit long before his savings are exhausted. See pages 66–8.

OTHER PERSONS RECEIVING RESIDENTIAL CARE
IN ENGLAND AND WALES

The obligation of local authorities to provide residential accommodation under section 21 of the National Assistance Act, 1948, for persons in need of care and attention not otherwise available to them applies not only to old people but to those in need of care and attention because of 'infirmity or any other circumstances'. Physically disabled people living in local authority, voluntary or private homes are therefore treated in the same way, for supplementary benefit purposes, as old people in similar accommodation.

In the case of persons who are mentally handicapped or who are or have been suffering from mental illness, local authorities are required, under the Health Services and Public Health Act, 1968, to provide 'care and after-care', including residential accommodation where appropriate. The provisions of the Ministry of Social Security Act relating to persons in part III accommodation do not apply to those for whom accommodation is provided under the Health Services and Public Health Act, who should strictly be regarded as paying an inclusive charge for board and lodging (assuming that they receive full board), their requirements being assessed at 'such amount as may be appropriate'. (See page 58.) In practice, however, the local authority will make the same charge for the accommodation as if it were provided under part III of the National Assistance Act, and the Commission assesses the claimant's requirements at the part III rate: £6·75 per week, out of which he is left with £1·35 for personal expenses. Where lodgings are arranged by the hospital rather than by the local authority, the claimant's requirements are assessed on the normal board and lodging basis, including the usual allowance of £2·10 for personal expenses. If the board and lodging charge is high by local standards because special after-care is provided, the Commission will allow only the proportion attributable to board and lodging as such and will expect the local authority to accept responsibility for the after-care element.

Another category of claimants for whom local authorities have a responsibility to provide accommodation where necessary is expectant and nursing mothers and their babies. Accommodation in mother and baby homes may be provided under either part III of the National Assistance Act, 1948, or section 22 of the National Health Service Act, 1946. In the past this led to differences of treatment for supplementary benefit purposes, but it was recently decided that all cases should be treated on the part III basis, the claimant's requirements being assessed at £6·75 (including £1·35 pocket money) for herself and £1·90 (the normal scale rate) for the baby.

HOMES IN SCOTLAND

In Scotland, the duty of local authorities to provide residential accommodation for 'persons in need' is laid down in section 12 of the Social Work (Scotland) Act, 1968. Section 94 defines persons in need as those who

(a) are in need of care and attention arising out of infirmity, youth or age; or

(b) suffer from illness or mental disorder or are substantially handicapped by any deformity; or

(c) have been rendered homeless and are in need of temporary accommodation; or

(d) being persons prescribed by the Secretary of State who have asked for assistance, are, in the opinion of a local authority, persons to whom the authority may appropriately make available the services and facilities provided by them under the Act (this category can be ignored at present, since the Secretary of State has not made use of his power of prescribing persons for this purpose).

The power to provide the accommodation, conferred by section 59 of the Social Work (Scotland) Act, is much wider than under the National Assistance Act. Section 59 of the Act empowers local authorities either to provide the accommodation themselves or to make arrangements with voluntary homes or with private establishments run for profit. The charges to be made by local authorities for such accommodation, however provided, are the same as those laid down for part III accommodation in England and Wales, and the person's requirements for supplementary benefit purposes are calculated on the part III basis, as explained above.

If the accommodation is not provided by the local authority, either directly or by arrangement with a voluntary or private home, the claimant's requirements are assessed on the 'board and lodging' basis, but, as in similar cases in England and

Wales, if the home is registered under section 62 of the Social Work (Scotland) Act, the part III rates are applied unless the local authority has refused to accept responsibility on the grounds that the person is not a 'person in need'. In that event, the Commission is prepared to meet a charge for board and lodging of up to £2 above what would normally be regarded as a reasonable charge for the locality.

STUDENTS

A young person aged 16 or over whose resources are insufficient to meet his needs can normally claim supplementary benefit in his own right. Section 9(1) of the Ministry of Social Security Act, however, states that a person attending a school or receiving full-time instruction of a kind given in schools shall not be entitled to benefit, except that where there are exceptional circumstances justifying it the Commission may award benefit on a discretionary basis. Normally, therefore, a young person who is still at school or is taking, for example, a full-time GCE 'O' or 'A' level course at a technical college cannot claim benefit (if his parents are eligible for benefit, he will be treated as a dependant in assessing their benefit while he is under 19). Discretionary awards on grounds of 'exceptional circumstances' are rare and are generally made only when it does not seem reasonable to expect the claimant's parents to support him – e.g. if a child is severely disabled or if a schoolgirl has a child of her own. The fact that the parents have a low income is not regarded as sufficient justification for paying benefit to the child, since help with the cost of keeping a child at school after the minimum school-leaving age can be obtained from the local education authority in the form of an education maintenance allowance (a higher school bursary in Scotland).

Once a young person has left school and is not taking a full-time course 'of a kind given in schools', if he continues with further studies he is no longer disqualified from receiving supplementary benefit by section 9(1) of the Act. The Commission, however, is not normally prepared to pay benefit to full-time students, most of whom are supported by grants from local education authorities or other bodies. Those who do not qualify for a maximum grant because they or their parents can afford to provide at least part of their maintenance are anyway unlikely to be in need of supplementary benefit. If a student is refused a grant on educational grounds it would clearly be anomalous that the Commission should finance him through a course of studies which the educational authority does not consider worthy of support from public funds. A student applying for supplementary benefit during his course, therefore, is normally refused benefit on the grounds that he is not available for work. Even if he is prepared to register at the employment exchange, benefit will still be refused, the fact that he is a student being regarded as an exceptional circumstance justifying the Commission in withholding benefit under paragraph 4(1)(b) of schedule 2 of the Act.

There are, however, exceptions. The most common is the payment of benefit during vacations. Local education authorities have a discretionary power to make additional grants to prevent hardship during the vacations, and before claiming supplementary benefit the student will be expected to apply for a hardship grant. If this is refused, and provided that the student registers for employment, he can claim benefit until he finds a job. During the Christmas and Easter vacations, when students can offer their services for only a few weeks, they are expected to accept any reasonable offer of work, even if it does not use their qualifications. In the longer summer vacation, they should be given an opportunity of seeking more suitable work before being expected to take an unskilled job. In assessing a student's resources, the Commission takes into account the fact that part of his normal grant is intended to meet vacation expenses (details of the component elements of the grant are normally given when it is awarded, but the local authority or other grant-giving body can be asked to supply this information at any time). This can cause difficulties, because a student who expects to take a job during the vacation is unlikely to have much of his grant left by the end of term. The Commission, however, takes the view that if a student spends during the term money intended for the vacation he cannot expect to have it replaced. This applies not only during the course of studies but at the end of it, since grants are normally awarded for the year from 1 September to 31 August. Thus, if the course ends in July and the student then registers for employment and claims supplementary benefit, his benefit entitlement up to the end of August will be reduced by the weekly equivalent of the allowance included in his grant for the vacations.

The second type of case in which students may receive supplementary benefit is where a student taking a first degree or equivalent course has dependants for whom no allowance is made in his grant, either because he has married during the course or because he has a child born more than six months after the start of the course. Local education authorities can award dependants' allowances on a discretionary basis in these circumstances. If they refuse to do so, the Commission will consider an award of supplementary benefit to the student to enable him to provide for his dependants if he would otherwise have no alternative but to give up his studies. The amount of benefit awarded will not exceed the weekly equivalent of the discretionary allowance that the education authority could have paid, and an award of this kind will not be made to any of the following:

(a) A postgraduate student;

(b) A student who does not have a local education authority grant for his own maintenance;

(c) A student whose only dependant is a wife who is capable of working.

Other cases occur from time to time in which a student's grant is not sufficient to maintain him or his dependants. This may be because the student's parents refuse to make the contributions towards his maintenance that have been assumed in calculating his grant. Or it may be that no allowance was made in the grant for his wife on the grounds that she was working and therefore not dependant on him, but she is temporarily sick or unemployed and not entitled to national insurance benefits. The Commission is not normally prepared to assist in cases of this sort, unless the need is urgent and hardship may result from a refusal. If the education authority is also unable or unwilling to help, it may be worth considering an appeal to the supplementary benefit tribunal.

Although, with the exceptions mentioned above, full-time students cannot normally claim supplementary benefits, the Commission adopts a slightly more flexible attitude towards unemployed young people engaging in part-time studies during normal working hours. If it can be shown that they are available for full-time employment, they may be allowed to draw supplementary benefit without giving up their studies. This is particularly important for young people in areas where jobs are temporarily hard to find, who enrol for a part-time course at the local technical college or elsewhere rather than remain totally idle. The Commission has agreed that they may receive benefit if the following conditions are satisfied:

(a) The college principal agrees that the student may abandon the course at any time;

(b) The student continues to register for employment and shows himself willing to accept any offer of suitable work and attend interviews for jobs;

(c) He has not given up his job voluntarily or abandoned a full-time course for a part-time course;

(d) The course does not take up more than three working days a week.

GOING ABROAD

Entitlement to supplementary benefit is limited by section 4 of the Ministry of Social Security Act to persons in Great Britain. Benefit is therefore not payable for any period during which the claimant is out of the country, whatever the reason for his absence. It should be noted that Great Britain does not include Northern Ireland, the Isle of Man or the Channel Islands.

It occasionally happens that a person in receipt of supplementary benefit has the opportunity of going abroad for a short time. For instance, a mother and her children may be invited to spend a holiday with relations in Ireland or on the continent. Although the Commission cannot pay benefit while she is abroad, it can, in appropriate cases, make an exceptional needs payment either before she leaves or after she returns. In practice, the Commission is usually prepared to make such a payment on the claimant's return, to meet any arrears of rent (or mortgage interest) and rates that have accrued in respect of the period of absence. What it will not do is to make such a payment in advance in order to prevent the arrears from accruing, or even to give a definite undertaking in advance that a payment will be made. The Commission argues that the decision to make an exceptional needs payment cannot properly be taken until the need – in this case the rent arrears – actually exists.

The Commission's policy on this question seems needlessly restrictive. The intention of going abroad for a short time (provided that there was good reason for doing so) could be regarded as creating an exceptional need for cash to meet fixed commitments such as rent for the period of absence. Since there will anyway be a saving of public funds in respect of the claimant's other living expenses, which the Commission will not be called upon to meet while he is abroad, it seems reasonable to suggest that generous use should be made of the discretionary power to make a lump-sum grant, without waiting for debts to accrue.

If the claimant's children are to remain behind in Britain in the care of another person, it will not normally be possible for their needs to be met by the Commission during the claimant's absence. The social services department (social work department in Scotland) of the local authority may, however, be prepared to help, either by receiving the children into care for the period in question or by giving financial help to prevent the need for reception into care, provided that they are satisfied that the parents' absence is justified.

COMING FROM ABROAD

It is not a condition for claiming supplementary benefit that the claimant should be of British nationality or normally resident in Great Britain. All that is required is that he should be in Great Britain during the period for which benefit is claimed. This does not mean, however, that foreign visitors who find themselves short of money can claim supplementary benefit in the same way as a person resident in Great Britain. Visitors from abroad must satisfy the immigration authorities that they are able to maintain themselves during their proposed stay before permission to enter is granted. If their money runs out, they are expected to return home rather than remain in Britain as a burden on public funds. Moreover, foreign visitors are normally forbidden, as a condition of entry, from taking employment, which means that they cannot register for work, as they would normally be required to do as a condition of receiving benefit.

Nevertheless, the Commission recognizes that it has a duty to prevent hardship, and, where urgent need exists, benefit can be paid under section 13 of the Ministry of Social Security Act. If a visitor is taken ill or for some other reason it would not be appropriate to make benefit conditional on registration for work, payments can be made in the normal way without resorting to the urgent need provisions of section 13, though such payments will continue only for as long as is necessary to allow other arrangements to be made.

A person arriving from abroad with a work permit, or who acquires one after arrival, is entitled to claim supplementary benefit if he is temporarily unable to work, subject to the usual condition of registration for work where appropriate. He will not, however, be able to claim benefit in respect of any dependants who are not in Great Britain.

REPATRIATION OF IMMIGRANTS

Under the Immigration Act, 1971, people who have come to the United Kingdom from abroad with the intention of settling permanently but who wish to resettle in an overseas country can, in certain cases, be helped with the cost of travel for themselves and their dependants – but not to a European country. The scheme is administered on behalf of the government by a voluntary body, International Social Service of Great Britain (ISS), which must satisfy itself that the proposed departure from the United Kingdom is likely to be in the best interests of the immigrant and any family concerned. Before the ISS scheme commenced, the Supplementary Benefits Commission occasionally made exceptional needs payments for this purpose, and it still does so. Payment of the cost of travelling to a European country is not excluded. In other respects, however, the circumstances in which the Commission will make grants towards the cost of repatriation are considerably narrower than those in which the ISS scheme can be used. The *Supplementary Benefits Handbook* lists the following conditions which must be satisfied by a claimant before a payment of this kind will be made:

(1) he has virtually no prospect of settling down and making a success of life in this country, whether because of physical or mental handicap or sickness or for other reasons (excluding a temporary high level of unemployment in the locality);

(2) he is unlikely to be able to find work and save up the fare, and the money is not available from any other source;

(3) he genuinely wishes to return home with his dependants, if any, and it seems to be in his own interests that he should do so;

(4) payment of the fare will lead to an ultimate saving in public funds.

The Commission will only help people who are already in receipt of supplementary benefit and, the *Handbook* adds, 'nobody who is capable of working and supporting himself is helped to pay for repatriation'.

179

The conditions under which help can be obtained through the ISS scheme are less stringent in two respects:

(a) A person with a poor employment record and/or prospects may be assisted even if he is not actually unemployed, provided that the family's income is less than £2 above supplementary benefit level (if it is slightly higher than this, but the case presents 'special welfare need', part of the cost of travelling may still be paid);

(b) It is not necessary to show that repatriation will result in a saving of public funds.

Fuller details of the ISS scheme can be obtained by writing to International Social Service of Great Britain, Cranmer House, 39 Brixton Road, London SW9 6DD. The scheme has not been extensively publicized, since it is intended only for those who decide as a matter of genuinely free choice that they wish to leave the United Kingdom. The Home Office has therefore laid down as a general principle that nobody in an official position should draw the attention of any individual to the existence of the new scheme except in response to a specific inquiry. For the same reason ISS will only accept applications direct from the individuals concerned, not by referral from other agencies.

Chapter 8

SUPPLEMENTING FULL-TIME EARNINGS

Supplementary benefit cannot normally be paid to a person who is in full-time work. The vast majority of people in full-time work would anyway not qualify for benefit, since their earnings, together with family allowances, are well above the supplementary benefit scale. But there remains a minority of workers who either do not earn enough to meet their requirements or who need short-term help even though they would normally be able to manage on their earnings. In certain limited circumstances, they can claim supplementary benefit, usually to tide them over an emergency or during the interval between starting a job and drawing the first week's wages. There is also a small category of claimants – those with reduced earning capacity because of disability and not working under a contract of service – who can claim benefit on a regular basis. With this exception, supplementary benefit is not available as a regular weekly supplement to full-time earnings. This is not a policy laid down by the Commission under its discretionary powers, and therefore open to challenge before an appeal tribunal. It is a rule contained in the Ministry of Social Security Act itself. Section 8 states that, with the exceptions mentioned above, 'a person shall not be entitled to benefit for any period during which he is engaged in remunerative full-time work'.

The effect of the full-time work disqualification is that a family may be living on an income well below the level of their requirements as set out in the supplementary benefit scale and yet be unable to claim supplementary benefit. Since August 1971, however, another source of help has been available to families in this situation – the family income supplement. In this chapter, we shall first consider the limited circumstances in which the full-time work disqualification does not operate and supplementary benefit may therefore be payable. The final section of the chapter will describe in detail how the family income supplement works and who may claim it.

CASES OF URGENT NEED

Section 13 of the Ministry of Social Security Act empowers the Commission to pay benefit 'in an urgent case', even where the claimant is in full-time work. (See page 106.) There are two important points to be noted about this provision. First, in deciding how much benefit, if any, should be paid in a particular case under section 13, the Commission is not bound by the normal rules regarding the calculation of requirements and resources set out in schedule 2 of the Act. It can therefore pay benefit in an urgent case to persons whose resources are more than sufficient to meet their normal requirements. Thus, in an emergency situation, the Commission can make an immediate payment of benefit without first making detailed inquiries about the circumstances of the claimant. Where appropriate, emergency help can be given in kind under section 14 (see page 33).

The second point to be noted is that where benefit is paid to a person in full-time work 'in an urgent case' under section 13, and would otherwise not be payable, the Commission may decide that the whole or part of the benefit shall be recoverable, i.e. that it should take the form of an advance or loan rather than an outright grant. This can only be done, however, if the Commission is satisfied that, in the circumstances, recovery would be equitable; and the claimant can appeal to the tribunal against a decision that benefit is to be recoverable. Generally speaking, it will not usually be equitable to expect repayment unless the claimant's normal income is above supplementary benefit level or he expects to receive a payment from some other source and the need for benefit arises only from the fact that the money is not available at the time when it is needed.

The Commission adopts a rather narrow interpretation of 'an urgent case' for the purposes of section 13. 'This power', the *Handbook* states, 'is primarily intended to cover payments when a family might otherwise go short of food, e.g. after a fire, flood etc. or when a wage packet has been stolen.' It can also be used to meet exceptional needs of an urgent nature, such as fares to visit a seriously ill relative, if the money cannot be obtained from other sources. The Commission is, however, careful not to allow section 13 to become merely a way of circumventing the full-time work disqualification. Requests for grants for clothing and other purposes, for which an exceptional needs payment might be made to a person receiving benefit on a regular basis, will therefore be rejected automatically if the claimant is in full-time work unless the need is genuinely urgent in the sense that it cannot be deferred even for a few days or met in other ways.

PAYMENTS DURING THE FIRST FIFTEEN DAYS AFTER STARTING WORK

The regulations provide that the full-time work disqualification is not to apply during the first fifteen days after the claimant becomes engaged in remunerative full-time work. Thus a person who has had a period off work (or in part-time work) may claim benefit, or continue to receive benefit already in payment, for up to fifteen days. If he has merely changed jobs, with no interval between one full-time job and the next, he will not qualify under this regulation because one cannot 'become engaged' in full-time employment unless, immediately before, one was not so engaged.

The object of the 'first fifteen days' rule is to avoid hardship due to the fact that a person starting a new job normally has to wait at least a week for his first payment of wages. Where it is the custom of the trade to work 'a week in hand', the first week's wages are not paid until the end of the second week;

hence the period of fifteen days specified in the regulations. Payment of benefit during this period is subject to the usual rules regarding the calculation of requirements and resources, with one important exception: any payment of wages or other earnings is taken into account in full apart from the first £1 per week, although the normal disregard of earnings for a claimant who is not required to register at the employment exchange is £2. (See page 65.) (The full £2 disregard is allowed in the case of a claimant who, when not working, would not be required to register for employment, e.g. a woman with dependent children. In the case of a person returning to work after a strike, wages received in the first fifteen days are taken into account in full, with no disregard; see page 130.) The practice of disregarding only £1 of earnings has been adopted by the Commission under its discretionary powers to reduce benefit where there are exceptional circumstances – the exceptional circumstance in this case being merely the fact that the claimant is in full-time work. It could well be argued that this is an improper use of the Commission's powers, since the circumstances are not really exceptional. An appeal on these grounds, however, might not succeed, since the tribunal would probably take the view that the Commission's policy, if not strictly lawful, was nevertheless reasonable.

If the first wage payment is not due at the end of the week in which employment commences, the employer may be willing to pay a 'sub' – an advance which will be recovered out of subsequent payments of wages. The Commission expects the claimant to ask for a 'sub' before agreeing to pay benefit for the following week if

(a) His wages will be substantially higher than his requirements by supplementary benefit standards;

(b) He has worked for at least three days by the time the benefit pay-day is reached; and

(c) It is known that the particular employer is willing to give 'subs'.

Unless all three of these conditions are satisfied, the question of asking for a 'sub' should not arise, although any 'sub' that the claimant has actually received before claiming benefit, even though he might not have been expected to ask for one, will be taken into account in calculating the benefit payable. The policy of requiring claimants to accept 'subs' can cause both hardship and injustice; hardship because the repayment of the 'sub' in subsequent weeks may leave the claimant with an inadequate income which can no longer be supplemented once the fifteen days have expired, and injustice because a man who works 'a week in hand' will receive two weeks' wages when he leaves the job and the Commission will expect him to live on this for at least two weeks if he is then unemployed, despite the fact that he was not allowed to draw two weeks' benefit at the beginning of the job. There are, moreover, obvious objections to compelling a man to ask for a 'sub' as soon as he starts work. If there is any question of hardship being caused, the social security office should be informed of this and asked to pay benefit without requiring the claimant to ask for a 'sub'. If payment is still refused, the refusal will constitute grounds for an appeal.

The fifteen-day rule is designed to meet the needs of weekly paid workers. It can cause difficulties if the claimant is paid monthly. In one case of this kind, after the Commission had refused to pay benefit after fifteen days, the claimant appealed and the tribunal awarded benefit for a further two weeks on grounds of 'urgent need' under section 13 of the Ministry of Social Security Act. The chances of an appeal on these grounds succeeding cannot be rated very highly unless the refusal of benefit is likely to cause substantial hardship. Nevertheless the possibility of such an appeal is worth considering, especially where the circumstances of the case are likely to arouse the sympathy of the appeal tribunal.

The special provisions regarding recovery of benefit paid to strikers during the fifteen days after their return to work were described in Chapter 5. See pages 130–32.

DISABLED PERSONS WITH REDUCED EARNING POWER

The full-time work disqualification does not apply to disabled persons working on their own account ('otherwise than under a contract of service'), whose earning power is substantially reduced by their disability in comparison with that of other people doing similar work. This limited exemption makes it possible for a disabled person to take on work, on a self-employed basis, within his capacities without losing the whole of his supplementary benefit. The fact that such work must not be carried out under a contract of service ensures that there is no risk of employers taking on disabled workers and deliberately underpaying them in the knowledge that the Commission will supplement their wages.

PART-TIME WORK

Since a person in full-time work cannot normally claim supplementary benefit, it may in some circumstances be more profitable to work part-time and claim benefit than to work full-time. In comparing the advantages of full-time and part-time work, the possibility of claiming a family income supplement must be taken into account, since the supplement is available only where the claimant (or the man where a man and woman claim jointly) is working full-time. In practice, the choice is unlikely to arise except in the case of a woman with one or more dependent children, since a man would not normally be allowed to continue drawing supplementary benefit while remaining voluntarily in part-time work. A mother claiming supplementary benefit, however, would not be required to register for employment as a condition of receiving benefit so long as at least one of her children was under 16. If she chose to work full-time, she might qualify for a family income supplement. The comparison to be made, therefore, would be between full-time earnings plus FIS (if any), on the one hand, and part-time earnings plus supplementary benefit on the other.

The dividing line between full-time and part-time work is generally taken to be thirty hours: a person working thirty hours or more per week is regarded as working full-time. For the purposes of the FIS scheme, this definition is contained in the regulations and therefore applies regardless of the circumstances. (See pages 188–9.) The supplementary benefit regulations, on the other hand, do not define 'full-time work'. A person working thirty hours or more can therefore still be treated as in part-time work and eligible for supplementary benefit if the Commission so decides, provided that the hours worked are less than the normal full-time working week for the particular occupation. It may thus be possible for a mother who finds that, even with FIS, she is worse off in full-time work, to reduce her working week by a few hours and thereby qualify to be treated as a part-time worker and claim supplementary benefit instead of FIS. Before doing so, however, it is advisable to consult the local social security office and obtain definite confirmation of their willingness to treat the case in this way.

FAMILY INCOME SUPPLEMENT

The family income supplement scheme was introduced by the Family Income Supplements Act, 1970, and came into effect in August 1971. It can be regarded as a form of supplementary benefit for families with children where the breadwinner is in full-time work and therefore cannot claim supplementary benefit as such. The responsibility for deciding whether a claimant is entitled to FIS and, if so, at what rate, was placed on the Supplementary Benefits Commission, and appeals against the Commission's decisions go to the same appeal tribunals that deal with supplementary benefit appeals.

FIS differs from supplementary benefits in a number of ways. In particular:

(a) Although the Act lays down 'prescribed amounts' of income below which families of different sizes qualify for FIS, the amount they receive is not the full amount by which their income falls short of the prescribed amount but only 50 per cent of the deficit.

(b) While supplementary benefit is affected by changes from week to week in the claimant's financial situation or the composition of his household, FIS is normally awarded for a twenty-six-week period and, once awarded, continues in payment at the same rate for the whole of that period, regardless of any such changes.

(c) FIS, unlike supplementary benefit, does not include a specific allowance for rent. The fact that one family pays a higher rent than another does not affect their respective entitlements to FIS.

(d) The discretionary powers of the Commission and the appeal tribunals are far more limited under the FIS scheme. The regulations leave certain questions to the judgement of the Commission or of the tribunal, but there is nothing comparable to the provisions of the Ministry of Social Security Act which give the Commission wide powers to increase, reduce or withhold benefit where there are 'exceptional circumstances'.

The full-time work condition

With the single and very limited exception of disabled people working on their own account, supplementary benefit is never payable as a regular weekly addition to the income of persons in full-time work. FIS, on the other hand, is *only* payable to those in full-time work. It can be claimed by either a man or a woman. In the case of a married couple living together or an unmarried couple who are living as man and wife, the claim must be made jointly by both of them but the man must be in full-time work. The reason for this is that if the woman is in full-time work but the man is not, he will be eligible to claim supplementary benefit if their joint income is below their requirements. FIS is designed to cover those cases where, because of the full-time work disqualification, supplementary benefit cannot be paid.

The full-time work condition is laid down in section 1(1) of the Family Income Supplements Act, 1970, which requires that the claimant (or the man, where the claim is made by a couple) shall be 'engaged, and normally engaged, in remunerative full-time work'. A person who does not normally work full-time cannot, therefore, qualify for FIS merely by doing a few days' work. Equally, however, the fact that a claimant has been unemployed for a long period does not disqualify him provided that he is in work at the time of the claim.

Full-time work is defined in the regulations as not less than thirty hours of work per week. The work must be 'remunerative'. A claimant can be either an employee or self-employed, and self-employment counts as remunerative work even if it does not yield a profit, provided that it is intended to be profitable. A full-time hobby is not remunerative work; an unsuccessful business or profession may be.

Children included in the family

The second fundamental condition of entitlement to FIS is that there must be at least one child in the family, aged under 16 or still at secondary school, and at least partly maintained by the claimants. A child can be counted as a member of the family even if the claimants are not its parents, provided that they are making some contribution towards its maintenance (e.g. a child living in its grandparents' household can be treated for FIS purposes as a member of their family, but not if its parents are providing or paying for the whole of its requirements). There is only one exception: a foster child, boarded out by a local authority or approved voluntary body, does not count as a member of the foster parents' family, even if part of the cost of maintaining the child falls on them. Nor does any boarding-out allowance paid to the foster parents count as part of their income in calculating their FIS entitlement.

It may occasionally happen that a particular child could be included in more than one family; for instance, where two claimants living in the same household (but not as man and wife) both contribute to the child's maintenance. The regulations leave it to the claimants to come to an agreement as to which family the child shall be included in. If they cannot agree, the Commission or the appeal tribunal must decide. Once a child has been included in one family to whom a supplement has been awarded, the same child cannot be included in any other family claiming FIS during the period – normally twenty-six weeks – for which the first award was made.

Residence

To qualify for FIS, the family must be in Great Britain. Supplementary benefit is subject to a similar condition (see pages 176–7), but the fact that FIS is normally awarded for a twenty-six-week period complicates the question of who is or is not to be regarded as being in Great Britain for this purpose. The regulations require that the family should be 'ordinarily resident in the United Kingdom' and that one or both of its adult members should be actually resident in Great Britain. Both 'resident' and 'ordinarily resident' are terms which have been the subject of numerous legal decisions in relation to national insurance, income tax, etc., and any claimant who is refused FIS either because he is not resident in Great Britain or because he is not ordinarily resident in the United Kingdom, and who is in any doubt as to whether the refusal is justified, should obtain legal advice on this question. Generally speaking, anybody who is working full-time in Great Britain should have no difficulty in passing both the residence tests unless he is obviously here as a temporary visitor – and even then he will probably qualify if his home is in Northern Ireland. Thus a man who comes from Northern Ireland to work in Great Britain may be able to claim FIS even though his wife and children are temporarily absent; but a man coming to Great Britain and leaving his family behind in a country outside the United Kingdom will probably not be able

to claim, because a family, for FIS purposes, must be ordinarily resident in the United Kingdom.

Calculation of FIS

The supplement payable for a particular family is half the
amount by which the claimant's normal gross income (or,
where the claim is made by a couple, their combined normal
gross incomes) falls short of the 'prescribed amount', subject
to a maximum payment of £5 a week. From April 1972, the
prescribed amount for a family with one child is £20 a week.
A further £2 is added for each additional child, making £22
for a two-child family, £24 for a three-child family, and so on.
The prescribed amounts are the same for families with only
one parent, whether the other parent is dead or merely absent.
These figures may be increased by regulations from time to
time. If the difference between the normal gross income and
the prescribed amount is 20p or less, no supplement is payable.
Where a supplement is payable, it is always a multiple of 10p,
the figure being adjusted upwards if necessary.

Example:

(a) A married couple with three children have a normal gross
income of £23·80.

Prescribed amount	£24·00
Normal gross income	23·80
Deficiency	20p
FIS payable	Nil

(b) if the family's normal gross income were £21·50, the calculation would be as follows:

Prescribed amount	£24·00
Normal gross income	21·50
Deficiency	2·50

FIS payable – ½ of £2·50 = £1·25, rounded to £1·30

(c) If the normal gross income were less than £14·20, the family
would qualify for the maximum FIS award of £5 a week.

Assessment of normal gross income

Income from all sources is taken into account in full, with the following exceptions:

(a) The whole of an attendance allowance or constant attendance allowance payable to a disabled person under the national insurance, industrial injuries or war pensions schemes;

(b) The first £2 of a war disablement pension;

(c) Supplementary benefit or FIS;

(d) Boarding-out allowance paid to foster parents by a local authority or approved voluntary body.

No deductions are allowed for national insurance contributions, income tax, etc. The rules for computing normal gross income from various sources are laid down in regulation 2 of the Family Income Supplements (General) Regulations 1971 (Statutory Instruments, 1971, No. 226):

(i) *Wage or salary*. The general rule is that normal gross income in the form of wages or salary is to be 'calculated or estimated by reference to' the average for the five weeks preceding the claim in the case of a weekly wage, or for the last two months in the case of a monthly paid employee. In most cases, the Commission simply works out a weekly average on this basis. It may, however, decide that the average does not fairly represent the claimant's normal income as at the date of the claim. In that case, the words 'calculated or estimated by reference to' enable the Commission to make an appropriate adjustment for any special factor which may have distorted the average. The regulation, moreover, provides that the Commission (or the appeal tribunal) may have regard to the claimant's average earnings 'over such other period or periods as may appear to them to be appropriate in order properly to determine what is that person's normal weekly income therefrom'. This power to look beyond the particular period of five weeks or two months is not limited to particular types of case, but the regulation specifically mentions the following circumstances in which it may be appropriate to use it:

(a) Where a person has been working abnormally long or short hours;

(b) Where a person began work in a particular occupation shortly before the claim;

(c) Where earnings from the occupation normally fluctuate seasonally;

(d) Where a person is not working under a contract of service – i.e. is self-employed.

The Commission is thus by no means bound by the normal procedure of averaging earnings over the previous five weeks or two months. It is free to take either a longer or a shorter period, which may or may not include the weeks immediately preceding the claim. It must, however, calculate or estimate the normal gross income from earnings by reference to the claimant's average earnings over some period in the past. It cannot simply estimate his present earning capacity without regard to past experience.

(ii) *Self-employment*. In assessing normal gross income from self-employment, the figure to be taken into account is net profit. The obvious period on which to base an estimate of weekly net profit is the last year for which accounts (preferably audited or accepted by the Inspector of Taxes for income tax purposes) are available. This basis will normally be accepted by the Commission. If the claimant's current income is lower than that shown by his last accounts, however, an estimate should be made for a more recent period. Similarly, if the Commission has reason to think that the claimant is now doing much better than during the period covered by the accounts, it will be justified in asking for more recent figures.

(iii) *Other income*. No specific method of assessing income other than earnings is laid down in regulation 2, which merely states that it is to be 'calculated or estimated on such basis as appears to the Commission or the Appeal Tribunal to be appropriate in the circumstances of the particular case'. Income derived from capital – dividends, interest, etc. – is taken into account in full, generally by dividing the annual sum by fifty-two to arrive at a weekly income figure. Income from boarders is normally taken into account on the basis that one fifth of the weekly payments represents net profit. If the profit from boarders is a main source of family income, however, detailed figures are required in the same way as for any other business. Rent received from sub-tenants is included in gross income after deducting 50p a week for wear and tear if the accommodation is sub-let unfurnished and £1 if it is furnished, and after appropriate deductions for the cost of electricity, gas and other services.

The most difficult types of income to assess are those which are received irregularly. The method adopted in most cases is to take an average over whatever period seems reasonable. A typical example is that of a separated wife or unmarried mother receiving irregular maintenance payments from her husband or the child's father. The Commission's policy in these circumstances is to take an average of the payments made over a period of generally not less than six months.

Claims and awards

A claim for FIS must be made on the official form (originally form FIS 2, now FIS 1), obtainable from any post office or social security office together with a pre-paid envelope addressed to the Department of Health and Social Security, Norcross, Blackpool FY5 3TD. Claim form FIS 1 is attached to a leaflet which gives a brief description of the scheme, including the current 'prescribed amounts' and some examples (as always with such leaflets, it is advisable to check that the latest edition is supplied; otherwise the information may be out of date).

With the exception of claims for renewal of a supplement, which can be made at any time during the four weeks before or after the expiry of the previous award, a FIS award can only be made from the pay-day on or following the date on which the claim is received. Any delay in sending in a claim will therefore usually result in some loss of benefit, though it may sometimes be worth losing a week's benefit in order to qualify for a larger supplement for the next twenty-six weeks, e.g. where the current week's earnings are expected to be far lower than those of five weeks ago, thus reducing the weekly average. In most cases, however, the initial claim should be made as soon as possible. If some of the information requested on the claim form is not immediately available, a note to this effect should be made on the form. If precise figures cannot be supplied at once, estimated figures should be entered and the fact that this has been done should be stated clearly on the form. Similarly, if pay slips or other evidence of earnings are not available or cannot be obtained without delay, the claim should be sent in with whatever supporting documents are to hand. Even if the claim is regarded as defective because the form has not been properly completed, the supplement can still be awarded as from the date of the claim, at the discretion of the Secretary of State, provided that the defects are remedied within a month.

A married couple or a man and woman living together as man and wife must make a joint claim – i.e. both of them must sign the claim form – unless, in the particular case, the Secretary of State accepts a claim by only one of them because he is satisfied that it would be unreasonable to require a joint claim. The requirement of a joint claim might, for instance, be waived if one of the two persons was mentally or physically incapable of managing his or her own affairs.

If the claim is successful, a supplement will normally be awarded for twenty-six weeks, regardless of any change of circumstances during that period (but see pages 196–7). Thus a family can continue drawing FIS for twenty-six weeks even if their income for most of the time is far above the prescribed amount. Changes in the composition of the household will also not affect the supplement once it has been awarded. For example, a child may cease to be dependent or a woman claimant may marry or cohabit with a man, but these changes will make no difference to the FIS payments until the current award expires and a new claim is made, when the family's circumstances at that time will be taken into account in deciding whether the supplement should be renewed. Even the death of a claimant will not extinguish the remaining payments under the award, provided that a suitable person is available to receive them and apply them for the benefit of the surviving members of the family.

FIS is paid weekly on Tuesdays (the same day as family allowances), by means of a book of orders which can be cashed at the post office. The first payment will be due on the Tuesday of or following the claim. In the case of a joint claim, the money can be drawn from the post office by either the man or the woman.

The Commission or the appeal tribunal may decide that a supplement should be paid for a period of less than twenty-six weeks, but not less than four weeks, if the available evidence leaves them in doubt as to the correct rate of payment but satisfies them that payment should be made at not less than a certain weekly rate. In these circumstances, the interim award must be at this minimum rate. For example, if the Commission decides that a supplement of at least £2 per week is payable but cannot decide whether the correct figure is more than this, it can make an award of £2 a week for a period of between four and twenty-five weeks, depending on how soon the situation is likely to be clarified sufficiently to enable a normal twenty-six-week award to be made. It should be noted that the maximum award of £5 a week cannot be made for less than twenty-six weeks since, if the Commission is satisfied that the correct rate of payment is not less than £5 it cannot be in doubt as to the precise amount payable.

Prevention of double payments

Although changes of circumstances during the period for which FIS has been awarded are normally ignored, there is one exception: where a person to whom a supplement is payable refuses or neglects to maintain any other person who was included in the family for FIS purposes and, as a result, the requirements of that other person have to be taken into account in a claim for supplementary benefit. A typical example would be where a man in receipt of FIS deserts his wife and children and, as a result, the wife applies for supplementary benefit. She would be allowed to continue cashing the FIS orders (the value of which would be deducted from any supplementary benefit payable to her), but the husband would no longer be allowed to do so. Similarly, if an unsupported mother in receipt of FIS deserts her children and their grandparents take them in and receive an increase in their supplementary pension in respect of them, the mother will no longer be entitled to draw FIS. This rule, however, only applies where a payment of supplementary benefit results from the failure to maintain. Otherwise, if the children are looked after by friends or relatives or taken into the care of the local authority, the parents can continue to draw FIS for the duration of the current award.

Another way in which double payments could occur is where a person who has been counted in one family for FIS purposes becomes a member of another family. Section 8(1) of the Family Income Supplements Act, 1970, therefore provides that where FIS is in payment for a family, no person who was included in that family at the time of the FIS claim can, during the period of the award, be treated as a member of another family.

Chapter 9

THE APPEAL TRIBUNAL

Any claimant who is dissatisfied with a decision of the Supplementary Benefits Commission can appeal to the local Supplementary Benefit Appeal Tribunal. The proportion of dissatisfied claimants who actually do appeal is very small. Yet the appeal machinery is easy to use, the hearings are on the whole friendly and informal, and the chances of success are reasonably good provided that there are genuine grounds for an appeal and that the facts and arguments are presented clearly to the tribunal. The object of this chapter is to explain how the machinery works and how to make the best use of it.

THE TRIBUNAL

There are 120 local Supplementary Benefit Appeal Tribunals in Great Britain. Each large city has at least one tribunal, but people living in small towns or rural areas may have to travel some distance to a tribunal hearing (travelling expenses are paid; see page 213).

There are normally three tribunal members at any hearing – the chairman and two others. The chairman is selected by the Secretary of State for Social Services from a panel of chairmen appointed by the Lord Chancellor. Of the other two members, one is 'appointed from among persons appearing to the [Secretary of State] to represent work-people', suitable nominations being supplied by the Trades Council Federation. The third member is appointed by the Regional Office of the Department of Health and Social Security from lists of persons put forward by local social security offices, local authorities, Citizens' Advice Bureaux, religious organizations, etc.

It is from this third category of tribunal members that the

chairmen are often appointed. The tribunal members attend appeal hearings on a rota basis, but the chairman normally sits more frequently than the other members. He is thus usually the most experienced member of the tribunal and the only one able to ensure that its decisions are reasonably consistent.

It is difficult to say just how independent the tribunal really is. The tribunal members certainly think of themselves as independent of both the Commission and the Department of Health and Social Security. The fact that the Department plays an active part in the selection process and that the clerk of the tribunal is an officer of the Department, however, is hardly calculated to reinforce the impression of independence.

THE POWERS OF THE TRIBUNAL

Section 18 of the Ministry of Social Security Act sets out the questions regarding supplementary benefit on which an appeal can be made to the tribunal. They are as follows:

(a) The right to or amount of any benefit.

(b) The payment of benefit to a person other than the claimant. See pages 33 and 55.

(c) The imposition of a condition under section 11 or section 12(2) (registration for employment or attendance at a course of instruction or training as a condition of receiving a supplementary allowance). See page 28.

(d) The provision of goods or services instead of the whole or part of any payment (i.e. benefit in kind). See page 33.

(e) The recovery of benefit paid in an urgent case to a person in full-time work. See pages 182–3.

(f) The amount which may be deducted from national insurance and other benefits, under section 16, in respect of supplementary benefit already paid for the same period. See pages 32–3.

The appeal can be either against a determination of the Commission on any of these matters or against a refusal by the Commission to review such a determination.

The supplementary benefit tribunals also deal with appeals

under the Family Income Supplements Act, 1970, section 7 of which provides that an appeal can be made against any determination of the Commission under the Act (i.e. a decision as to the right to or amount of a family income supplement or, exceptionally, the period for which it is payable) or a refusal to review such a determination where a review is permitted under the regulations. Unlike supplementary benefit, FIS is not affected by a change of circumstances during the period for which it was awarded (normally twenty-six weeks). Refusal to review a supplement following a change of circumstances does not, therefore, constitute grounds for an appeal.

In deciding an appeal, the tribunal is free to make any decision which would have been within the powers of the Commission. In FIS cases, the tribunal will generally be concerned with questions of fact as to whether a claimant is in full-time work, what is the family's normal gross income, etc. Supplementary benefit appeals, on the other hand, are very often about the use of the Commission's discretionary powers; and even if the use of discretion is not the subject of the appeal, it is always present in the background, since there are few cases in which it cannot be used by either the Commission or the tribunal to modify the normal operation of the Act. The tribunal thus has very wide powers indeed, in supplementary benefit cases, to interpret the intentions of Parliament. Moreover, unlike the Commission's officers, it is not bound in any way by any policy decisions the Commission may have taken regarding the use of its discretionary powers. It does not have access to the confidential instructions issued to officers in documents such as the 'A Code'. It may of course be aware of the Commission's policies as published in the *Handbook* and elsewhere, but it is not obliged to comply with those policies, either generally or in a particular case. On the contrary, the tribunal has a duty to apply its own judgement to the circumstances of the case, even if this results in a decision which is totally at variance with the policy and practice of the Commission.

The tribunal has the power to reduce as well as increase benefit. In practice, however, appeals hardly ever result in a reduction of benefit, and the risk of this occurring should certainly not deter anybody with a reasonable case from using the appeal machinery.

The tribunals, like the Commission, must of course operate within the provisions of the Ministry of Social Security Act or the Family Income Supplements Act and the regulations made under those Acts. Beyond this, they seldom have to consider questions of law as such; indeed, they would have difficulty in doing so, since few tribunal members are qualified lawyers and they do not have access to legal advice during appeal hearings. Occasionally, however, the tribunals have to decide questions on which, in other contexts, relevant decisions have been made by the Courts. Both the Commission and the tribunal must have regard to such precedents, though in practice they do not always do so.

WHEN TO APPEAL – AND WHEN NOT TO

If a decision by the Commission seems wrong or ungenerous, the first step to take in most cases is to ask the local office to reconsider it. Requests of this kind generally carry more weight if made through an organization which is known to be knowledgeable on social security matters – e.g. a trade union, claimant's union, social work agency, or the local branch of the Child Poverty Action Group – or through an individual such as the local M.P., a local councillor or a clergyman. Whether the request is made by the claimant himself or by somebody else on his behalf, it is best to put it in writing (and remember to keep a copy) or, if the matter is urgent, to telephone. Calling at the local office is not advisable, as it is often difficult to get past the official on the counter to a senior officer without creating a good deal of fuss. The more senior the officer dealing with the matter, the easier it will be for him to alter the original decision. Hence, when telephoning, it is advisable to ask for the manager or the deputy manager (the officer dealing with the particular case will anyway often be out of the office).

The claimant is not usually given any detailed explanation of how his benefit, or the decision that he is not entitled to benefit, was arrived at. The local office must, however, supply such an explanation in writing if requested to do so. If the query is about the amount of weekly benefit, a 'notice of assessment' (form A 124A) should be requested. Asking for a written explanation will often avoid the need for an appeal, either because the claimant is satisfied with the explanation or because the request itself leads to a reconsideration of the decision or merely to the correction of an arithmetical error.

If a decision is revised in the claimant's favour, without recourse to the appeal tribunal, he is entitled to arrears in respect of any underpayment of benefit under the original decision. For instance, if benefit has been restricted because the claimant's rent was considered unreasonable and this decision is subsequently revised, arrears should be paid for the whole period of the restriction, unless the new decision is based on a genuine change of circumstances rather than a change of mind on the part of the Commission.

In some cases it is best to lodge an appeal straight away, without attempting to get the decision changed by the local office. One such case is where a supplementary allowance is refused under the 'four-week rule'. (See pages 140–45.) Since it is the Commission's policy, in this situation, to continue payment of benefit at a reduced rate until the appeal hearing, it is obviously advisable to appeal at once. An immediate appeal is also advisable where it is known that the local office has acted in accordance with the Commission's stated policy and is therefore unlikely to revise its decision, or where for any other reason negotiation with the local office seems unlikely to produce results.

Once a claimant has decided to appeal, he should do so without further delay. An appeal must be lodged within twenty-one days of the notification of the decision 'or within such further time as the chairman may for good cause allow'.

Undue delay may therefore result in a refusal to hear the appeal. If an appeal is lodged more than twenty-one days after notification of the decision, the reason for the delay should be explained clearly. Chairmen are in practice usually prepared to hear late appeals, provided that there is a reasonable explanation of the delay.

The twenty-one-day limit for lodging an appeal can sometimes be circumvented by first asking the Commission to review the decision. Under the regulations, a decision can be reviewed only if it was 'made in ignorance of, or was based on a mistake as to, some material fact', or there has been a change of circumstances since the decision was made which would affect the amount of benefit payable in any week by more than 10p. There is no power to review a decision if it was made in full knowledge of the facts and there has been no relevant change of circumstances. Where a decision is reviewed, the outcome of the review will be a new decision, even if its effect is to confirm the old one, and an appeal may be lodged against the new decision within a further twenty-one days. If the grounds for the review are that the decision was made in ignorance of, or based on a mistake as to, a relevant fact, the review will cover the whole period during which benefit was paid on the basis of that decision; and an appeal against the review decision will allow the amount of benefit payable for the whole period to be considered by the tribunal. If the review is due to a change of circumstances rather than to an error of fact underlying the original decision, only the period since the change occurred will be reconsidered. In either case, however, it may be possible to reopen matters which were decided far more than twenty-one days previously. The Commission is not obliged to review a decision even where it has the power to do so, but a refusal will itself constitute grounds for an appeal.

HOW TO APPEAL

Lodging an appeal is extremely simple. An official form for this purpose can be obtained on request from the local social security office but, as it is quite unnecessary to use the form, there seems little point in going to the trouble of obtaining it. All that is required is that notice of the appeal should be given in writing at an office of the Department of Health and Social Security – any office will do, but it avoids confusion if the appeal is sent to the office which made the disputed decision.

The notice of appeal should state clearly what the appeal is against: e.g. 'I appeal against the decision of the Supplementary Benefits Commission to cut off my supplementary allowance', or 'I appeal against the refusal of the Supplementary Benefits Commission to grant me an exceptional needs payment for the purchase of an overcoat', or 'I appeal against the amount of the payment granted to me by the Supplementary Benefits Commission for the cost of my husband's funeral', or 'I appeal against the refusal of the Supplementary Benefits Commission to meet my rent in full'. The notice of appeal can be addressed to the Manager, Department of Health and Social Security. It must be signed by the claimant himself. If it is late (more than twenty-one days after the decision was notified), the notice should explain why.

There is no need at this stage to give a more detailed explanation of the grounds of the appeal, and most people will find it more convenient to do this at the hearing. On the other hand, there may sometimes be advantages in setting out the arguments more fully in the notice of appeal since, as explained below, the case will be re-examined by the Commission before it reaches the tribunal and, if the claimant's arguments are sufficiently convincing, there is a possibility of the decision being revised without the necessity of an appeal hearing. Besides, if the claimant has nobody to help him present his case at the hearing, he may find it easier to put it in writing beforehand, while the facts are fresh in his mind, than to explain it orally in the presence of the tribunal. It is a matter of judgement and personal preference, therefore, whether to confine the notice of appeal to the bare essentials or to go into detail. Whichever course is adopted, it is important that all the matters in dispute should be mentioned – e.g. 'I appeal against the reduction of my supplementary allowance under the wage stop *and* the refusal to meet my rent in full', rather than just one or the other – since the tribunal cannot consider a decision which falls outside the terms of the notice of appeal (tribunals sometimes do stray beyond their brief, but it is unwise to assume that they will do so).

Another point which can sometimes usefully be mentioned in the notice of appeal is the question of urgency. There is usually a delay of about a month (more in some areas, less in others) before an appeal comes before the tribunal. If serious hardship would be caused by such a long delay, it is worth adding to the notice of appeal 'Will you please arrange for this appeal to be heard as soon as possible?', together with a brief explanation of the reasons for the request. It should not be assumed that such a request will necessarily be complied with but, if the grounds seem genuine, the clerk of the tribunal will generally try to fit the case in at an early hearing.

BEFORE THE HEARING

During the interval of anything from two weeks to two months or more between the lodging of a notice of appeal and the tribunal hearing, the disputed decision is subjected to a thorough process of re-examination, which is described in a recent report published by the Child Poverty Action Group, *Supplementary benefits and the administrative review of administrative action*, by R. J. Coleman. First, the manager of the local social security office examines the case to see whether there are adequate grounds for reviewing and altering the decision without recourse to the tribunal. This may involve a visit by one of his officers to the claimant if there are points which need clarification. If a new decision is made, superseding the original one, the claimant is told that his appeal has lapsed, even though the new decision may still not give him all that he thinks he is entitled to. He is also told that he can appeal against the new decision if he still wants the matter considered by the tribunal.

Sometimes, where the appeal is about the amount of weekly benefit, a new decision is made but is not back-dated to cover the whole period since the original decision came into effect. In that case the appeal will go forward to the tribunal unless the claimant decides to withdraw it – and there is no reason why he should do so if he is still not satisfied.

If the review by the local manager does not result in the decision being superseded, the case is then referred to the Commission's regional office, where a similar process takes place, which, once again, may lead to a new decision which may or may not supersede the original one. Finally, in a few cases involving important policy questions, the papers are referred to the Headquarters of the Commission, involving a further possibility of a new decision being made. Only if the original decision remains unaltered at the end of this process, or a new decision has been made covering only part of the relevant period, will the appeal reach the stage of a tribunal hearing – and, even then, only if the claimant has not decided to withdraw it meanwhile.

Coleman found that, in the twelve months ending in October 1969, more than one in five of the appeals lodged resulted in a new decision being made, usually by the local office, which either superseded the original decision or led to the claimant withdrawing his appeal. In addition one in every nine appeals was withdrawn by the claimant although the original decision remained unchanged. Altogether, therefore, about a third of all appeals never reached the tribunal because they were either superseded or withdrawn before the hearing. No doubt some of the claimants concerned were either satisfied with the new decision or convinced that their appeal was, after all, not justified. But there must certainly have been others who decided not to go ahead because, although still not satisfied that they were being correctly treated, they were grateful for being given something extra and possibly feared that the tribunal might reduce their benefit rather than increase it.

There is obviously no point in insisting on an appeal going to the tribunal if it can be settled to the claimant's satisfaction without a formal hearing. But, equally, there is no reason why any claimant should feel obliged to abandon an appeal simply because he has been given part of what he is claiming, and still less because he has been told by an officer of the Commission that his appeal stands no chance of succeeding. In particular, where a new decision supersedes the original one and the appeal therefore lapses, there should be no hesitation in appealing against the new decision if it is still not satisfactory.

HELP WITH APPEALS

The appeal machinery has been kept as simple and informal as possible, since most claimants have little or no help in preparing their case and presenting it to the tribunal. Nobody should be afraid of appealing simply because they have nobody to help or advise them. The tribunals are used to dealing with claimants who have no expert knowledge and who are nervous and inarticulate. Indeed, the nervous and inarticulate claimant may well get a more sympathetic hearing.

Nevertheless, if expert advice and help are available, it generally pays to make use of them. Trade union members may find that their union can help. Otherwise, the most likely source of help will probably be either a local claimants' union or a branch of the Child Poverty Action Group. Any of these bodies should be able to offer useful advice on whether there are sufficient grounds for an appeal, on the wording of the notice of appeal, and on the presentation of the case at the tribunal hearing. They may also be willing to attend the appeal hearing as a 'representative' of the claimant and present the case to the tribunal on his behalf, as a solicitor or barrister would do in court.

One of the differences between this kind of tribunal and a law court is that legal aid is not available for tribunal proceedings. A few solicitors are prepared occasionally to represent claimants at tribunal hearings for nothing, but for most claimants this kind of help is not available. They can, however, get legal advice before the hearing under the Legal Aid and

Advice Scheme. This entitles anybody on supplementary benefit, whose savings, if any, do not exceed £125, to obtain free advice (an interview can last up to 1½ hours). A person not receiving supplementary benefit but whose income and savings are small can get the same service for 12½p, or, if his income or savings are too high to qualify, he can get half an hour's advice for £1 under the Voluntary Legal Advice Scheme if the solicitor agrees. Details of the schemes and a list of local solicitors who operate them can be obtained from a Citizens' Advice Bureau, the local court offices or any solicitor's office. At present, these arrangements are limited to the giving of advice but, under the '£25 scheme' to be introduced in the near future, solicitors will be able to provide other kinds of help to supplementary benefit claimants and other people with low incomes, either free or at a reduced fee. The £25 scheme, however, will not cover representation at appeal hearings.

A solicitor will obviously be qualified to advise on the legal aspects of an appeal. In most supplementary benefit appeals, however, the issues involved are only partly matters of law, and the non-legal aspects are often more important. It may be more helpful, therefore, to get advice from one of the organizations mentioned above which specialize in this field. Although their workers are usually not lawyers, they are often more knowledgeable about the policies and practices of the Supplementary Benefits Commission than the average solicitor. They are usually in touch with lawyers who can advise on the legal aspects of the case.

Unfortunately there is no easy way of finding out what is the best local source of advice and help. Organizations, however well-intentioned, which offer this kind of help may not have local members who are really qualified to give it. It is therefore advisable, when approaching them, to ask (as politely as possible) how much practical experience they have had of supplementary benefit tribunals. It may also be worth asking about local sources of help at the Citizens' Advice Bureau (the CAB itself will advise on appeals if asked, but is unlikely to have much specialized knowledge of the subject).

THE TRIBUNAL HEARING

Notification of the time and place of the hearing usually reaches the claimant five or six days before the hearing. It is accompanied by a form (B/O. 22 for a supplementary benefit appeal; FIS 64 for a family income supplement appeal) giving the following particulars:

(a) The date on which the appeal was lodged;

(b) The decision against which the claimant is appealing and the date on which the decision was issued;

(c) The 'appellant's statement' – i.e. a copy of the notice of appeal;

(d) 'Observations by officer of the Commission' – i.e. any statement the Commission wishes to make in explanation or defence of its decision;

(e) Details of the calculation of the claimant's weekly benefit (these details are usually given even if the result is 'nil').

Copies of this form are supplied to each member of the tribunal and its contents form the basis of the hearing.

Appeal hearings take place in private. Unlike most other kinds of tribunal hearings, neither the public nor the press is admitted. Those present may include the following:

(a) The members of the tribunal. If one of the three members is missing, the hearing can still go on provided that the chairman is present and that neither the claimant nor the officer representing the Commission objects to the case being heard by an incomplete tribunal.

(b) The tribunal clerk, who is an officer of the Department of Health and Social Security temporarily seconded for this purpose. He is responsible for arranging tribunal hearings, distributing papers (including form B/O. 22 or FIS 64), paying expenses, keeping a record of the proceedings at the hearing, and notifying the claimant of the tribunal's decision and the reasons for it.

(c) The claimant (or, as he is called for this purpose, the 'appellant'). If he does not turn up, the hearing may, and usually does, take place in his absence.

(d) Not more than two persons accompanying or representing the claimant. The claimant's representatives may attend the hearing and speak on his behalf even if he himself is not present.

(e) With the tribunal's permission, any adult whose requirements and resources are, were, or may be aggregated with those of the claimant under paragraph 3 of schedule 2 of the Ministry of Social Security Act. In most cases this would mean the claimant's wife.

(f) Not more than two persons representing the Commission. Usually only one officer of the Commission attends, known as the 'presenting officer'.

(g) Witnesses called by either side.

(h) With the chairman's consent, not more than two other persons 'if he is satisfied that they are persons who are genuinely engaged in research connected with appeals to Appeal Tribunals or have other good and sufficient reasons for being present'. Such persons must have given the clerk reasonable notice in writing of their desire to be present and the reasons, and a written undertaking not to publish any information they obtain during the hearing in a way which would make it likely that individual claimants could be identified; and if the claimant is present at the hearing, he must be told of their wish to be present and the reasons and they will be allowed in only if the claimant does not object.

(j) A member of the Council on Tribunals or of the Scottish Committee of the Council.

In most cases, apart from the claimant, only the tribunal members, the clerk and the presenting officer are present, though it is becoming more common for claimants to be represented and, as the rule admitting research workers came into operation only in July 1971, they are also likely to appear with increasing frequency for some time to come.

Although an appeal may be heard in the absence of the claimant, the chances of success are generally greater if he attends the hearing. The notice of the time and place of the hearing will be accompanied by a form on which the claimant is asked to state whether he will be present. If there are good reasons why he cannot attend, such as illness or difficulty in taking time off work, these should be explained in writing when returning the form, or by the claimant's representative (if any) at the hearing. An adjournment of the hearing may be requested and will usually be granted in these circumstances, provided that the claimant is likely to be able to attend at a later date. If the claimant wishes to ask for an adjournment on other grounds, such as the need for more time to prepare his case, it is advisable for him to attend in person to make the request since, if he does so in writing and it is refused, the hearing will proceed in his absence.

If the tribunal is incomplete, the hearing can take place only if the claimant does not object. If the missing member is the trade union representative and the case is one in which his opinion and knowledge of local industrial conditions may be crucial, it may be worth insisting on the hearing being deferred. In most cases, however, the claimant is unlikely to suffer from the absence of one member of the tribunal; in fact, the two remaining members may be, if anything, more inclined to view the case sympathetically lest there should be any suspicion of bias resulting from the absence of the third member.

The proceedings of the tribunal are governed by rules made by the Secretary of State for Social Services after consultation with the Council on Tribunals. The present rules are the Supplementary Benefit (Appeal Tribunal) Rules 1971 (Statutory Instruments, 1971, No. 680) and the Family Income Supplements (Appeal Tribunal) Rules 1971 (Statutory Instruments, 1971, No. 622). Apart from stating who shall, or may, be present at a hearing, the rules provide that the claimant or his representative shall be entitled to be heard, to call witnesses, and to put questions directly to the presenting officer(s) and to any witnesses called by either side; and the presenting officer has similar rights, including that of putting questions directly to the claimant. The precise way in which the hearing is to be conducted, however, is left for the chairman to decide. The procedure therefore varies to some extent from one tribunal to another. Broadly speaking, it is usually something like this:

(a) The chairman assures the claimant that the tribunal is independent, and explains the procedure to him.

(b) The presenting officer reads out the contents of form B/0.22. This provides a useful opportunity for the claimant or his representative to put his notes and thoughts in order.

(c) The chairman invites the claimant or his representative to present his case. In doing so, the claimant or his representative may call witnesses and question them, or place any relevant documents before the tribunal.

(d) The chairman asks the presenting officer if he wishes to say anything. He may comment on the arguments put forward on behalf of the claimant or bring in new arguments. He may also call witnesses or put questions to the claimant or his witnesses. In most cases, however, the presenting officer makes only a few brief comments.

(e) The claimant or his representative may put questions to the presenting officer or his witnesses.

(f) An informal discussion follows, in which any member of the tribunal may put questions to the claimant, his representative, the presenting officer or the witnesses (if any – usually there are none). In practice, this stage of the hearing is seldom clearly defined since the tribunal members may intervene in any of the preceding stages.

(g) When the chairman is satisfied that all the relevant facts have been elicited, the claimant, his representative and the presenting officer are asked to withdraw. The clerk remains with the tribunal while they discuss the evidence and arrive at their decision.

(h) The claimant may be asked to wait outside and then invited back into the tribunal room with the presenting officer to be informed of the tribunal's decision. More usually, he is told that he will be informed of the decision by post in a few days. Whichever procedure is adopted, it is a requirement of the Tribunal Rules that a statement of the decision and of the reasons for the decision should be sent to the claimant by the clerk as soon as practicable after the decision is made.

(j) Either before or after the hearing, the clerk asks the claimant, any person accompanying or representing him, and any witnesses called by him whether they wish to claim travelling expenses or compensation for loss of earnings. Payment of these is subject to the discretion of the Secretary of State and an unreasonable claim would presumably not be met. Travelling expenses are, however, paid for representatives travelling a considerable distance to attend tribunal hearings. Compensation for loss of earnings is subject to a maximum of, at present, £4·75 per day. Subsistence expenses can also be paid if a lengthy absence from home is necessary.

PREPARING A CASE FOR THE TRIBUNAL

It is always advisable to work out in detail, a few days before the hearing, the arguments to be presented to the tribunal. This not only ensures that important points are not forgotten in the stress of the hearing. It also compels the claimant or his representative to think about the kinds of evidence needed to support their case. Usually the best time to do this is immediately after receiving form B/O.22 or FIS64, which sets out both the details of the appeal and the observations of the Commission. The form should be studied with care, the following points being particularly noted:

(a) Check that the decision appealed against is correctly and fully stated. Otherwise the tribunal may not deal with all the matters in dispute.

(b) Check the Commission's 'observations' for any factual errors. Also check, if possible, any references to the law (usually the Ministry of Social Security Act, 1966, or the Family Income Supplements Act, 1971, and the Regulations made under them), both for inaccuracies and for misleading omissions; for example, if regulation 6(1) of the Supplementary Benefit (Claims and Payments) Regulations, 1966, is quoted in support of the argument that claims cannot be back-dated, regulation 6(3), which permits back-dating where there are exceptional circumstances justifying it, should also be quoted.

(c) Check the calculation of benefit, noting particularly the treatment of resources and any discretionary additions or reductions which might be open to question.

(d) Watch for any ways in which the Commission's actions or arguments depart from the policies set out in the *Handbook* (or in earlier chapters of this book).

When considering what arguments and evidence to put forward at the hearing, it is important to remember that the tribunal members are not trained lawyers and are more likely to be swayed by sympathy (or lack of it) and common sense than by legal arguments, however brilliant. Once they are convinced that the appeal *deserves* to succeed, they will often find 'exceptional circumstances' to justify a favourable decision, whereas they might hesitate to make a similar decision on grounds of general principle. There are several reasons for this. Tribunal members tend to feel more confident about the use of their discretionary powers than about making decisions on grounds of principle or of law. If their decision is different from that of the Commission, they prefer to treat the difference as a matter of judgement rather than implying that the Commission's decision was wrong in principle. And, not least important, despite their theoretical independence, the tribunals tend to avoid making decisions which openly conflict with the Commission's policy and might therefore cause political embarrassment or, at least, invidious comparisons between the particular case under appeal and hundreds of other similar cases. For all these reasons, it is generally best to concentrate on the facts of the particular case and, above all, not to imply that it is in any way a 'test case' or that, by deciding in favour of the claimant, the tribunal will be casting doubt on the Commission's policy.

At the same time, it is often necessary to stress that the tribunal is not bound to apply the normal policy of the Commission to the particular set of circumstances under consideration. Tribunal members do not always draw a clear distinction between the provisions of the Act and regulations, which are binding on the tribunal, and the instructions issued by the Commission to its officers and summarized in the *Handbook*, which are not. For instance, in a case involving the 'four-week rule', it may be necessary to remind the tribunal that the 'rule' is not to be found anywhere in the Act but has been adopted as an administrative practice by the Commission, using its discretionary power to withhold benefit under paragraph 4(1) (b) of schedule 2 of the Act.

In presenting a case at a tribunal hearing, whether as a claimant or as a representative, it is helpful to deal with the following matters, at least to the extent that they are not adequately dealt with on form B/0.22 or FIS 64:

(a) Draw attention to any errors or mis-statements of *fact* on form B/0.22 or FIS 64.

(b) Describe briefly the claimant's circumstances – e.g. his normal occupation, how long he had been unemployed, sick, etc., what illness or disability he suffers from, and, if the claimant is a woman, whether she is unmarried, separated, divorced or widowed.

(c) Explain precisely what the appeal is about. If there are several points at issue, explain each separately.

(d) Present detailed arguments in favour of the appeal and rebutting the arguments used in the Commission's 'observations' on form B/0.22 or FIS 64. Bring any documentary evidence to the attention of the tribunal at the appropriate point in the presentation of the case (if long or complicated documents are to be produced as evidence, it may be helpful to pass them to the chairman before starting to address the tribunal – but short and simple documents which the tribunal can digest are generally more effective). Point out any respects in which the Commission has departed from its normal policy, as stated in the *Handbook* or elsewhere, to the detriment of the claimant.

(e) If possible, state exactly what decision the tribunal is being asked to make, including, where appropriate, the amount of arrears requested. The tribunal will find it easier to make a favourable decision if it has some definite figures before it rather than just a vague plea for more generous treatment. If what is being asked for is contrary to the Commission's normal practice, stress that it is within the Commission's (and, therefore, the tribunal's) powers, preferably quoting the relevant provisions of the Act or the regulations.

If the claimant or his representative is calling witnesses, it is advisable to ask the chairman at what point he would like them to give evidence, since the procedure varies from one tribunal to another. It is generally very informal and evidence is not taken on oath.

AFTER THE HEARING

The claimant normally receives the notification of the tribunal's decision from the clerk within two or three days. The notification must give the reasons for the decision and may also include a statement of the tribunal's findings on any questions of fact that arose during the hearing. The local social security office is informed of the decision at the same time and should take any necessary action to implement it without delay. If the statement of the tribunal's decision is ambiguous or does not cover all the matters which were the subject of the appeal, or if the reasons for the decision are not clearly explained, the clerk should be asked to provide a fuller statement.

Although section 18 of the Ministry of Social Security Act states that 'any determination of the Tribunal shall be conclusive for all purposes', there may sometimes be further steps which the claimant can take if he is still not satisfied. If the decision was correct in law and the objection is merely to the way in which the tribunal exercised its discretionary powers, the only possibility of obtaining a more favourable decision will be to wait until there has been a relevant change of circumstances and make a new claim, followed if necessary by a further appeal (the fact that the first appeal was rejected does not mean that it is pointless to appeal again, since there will probably be different people sitting on the tribunal at the second appeal hearing). Whatever decision is made on the new claim, whether by the Commission or by the tribunal, will operate only from the date of that claim.

A second possibility of getting the tribunal's decision revised arises where the decision was 'made in ignorance of, or was based on a mistake as to, some material fact'. In these circumstances, the Commission can be asked to review the tribunal's decision and to substitute a different decision in the light of the facts now available. The Commission's power to review its own decisions has already been mentioned. (See page 203.) It may seem odd that the Commission should also have power to review the decision of a tribunal, but this is indeed the case. The power can only be used, however, where the tribunal's decision was based on an error as to the facts, or there has been a subsequent change of circumstances. It cannot be used to correct an error of judgement on the part of the tribunal.

Finally, in rare cases, it may be possible to argue that the tribunal's decision is wrong in law. For example, in a case where 'cohabitation' is alleged, the tribunal may have adopted a definition of cohabitation which is clearly at variance with the findings of the Courts on this question. Where such an error of law has occurred, there may be grounds for applying to the Divisional Court for a 'prerogative order' of *mandamus* or *certiorari*. Legal aid can be granted for this purpose. The first step should always be to consult a solicitor under the Legal Aid and Advice Scheme or the Voluntary Legal Advice Scheme, or to seek legal advice from an organization specializing in matters of this kind (e.g. the Citizens' Rights Office, 1 Macklin Street, London WC2B 5NH, telephone number 01-405 9795).

SUPPLEMENTARY BENEFIT SCALES

	Weekly rate October 1972 £	Weekly rate November 1973 £
Ordinary scale		
Husband and wife	10·65	
Person living alone (householder)	6·55	
Any other person (non-householder) aged:		
Not less than 18	5·20	
Less than 18 but not less than 16	4·05	
Child aged:		
Less than 16 but not less than 13	3·40	
Less than 13 but not less than 11	2·75	
Less than 11 but not less than 5	2·25	
Less than 5	1·90	
Blind scale		
Husband and wife:		
If one of them is blind	11·90	
If both of them are blind	12·70	
Any other blind person aged:		
Not less than 18	7·80	
Less than 18 but not less than 16	4·95	
Less than 16 but not less than 13	3·40	
Less than 13 but not less than 11	2·75	
Less than 11 but not less than 5	2·25	
Less than 5	1·90	
Non-householder rent allowance	0·70	
Attendance requirements		
Higher rate	5·40	
Lower rate	3·60	
Long-term addition		
Aged 80 or over	0·85	
Aged under 80	0·60	

Appendix 2

EXAMPLES OF SUPPLEMENTARY BENEFIT ASSESSMENTS

The examples given below illustrate some of the more common types of case. To understand the calculations, it may be necessary to refer to the sections of the guide in which particular points are explained in detail. The relevant page numbers are shown on the right hand side.

EXAMPLE A

(i) The A. family consists of Mr and Mrs A. and their three children – Harold (19), who earns £12 a week, Joan (15), and Eric (13). They live in a council house, paying rent and rates of £6 a week, with no rent rebate. Mr A. is drawing sickness benefit of £16 a week. He has savings of £700 and Mrs A. has £260.

Requirements			*See page*
Mr and Mrs A.		£10·65	
Joan		3·40	
Eric		3·40	
Rent and rates	£6·00		
Less ¼ share attributed to Harold	1·50		41
		4·50	
		21·95	
Resources			
Sickness benefit		16·00	
Family allowances		90	
Assumed income from capital	£1·75		67–8
Less disregard	1·00		64
		75	
		17·65	
Supplementary allowance		£3·30	

219

(ii) After 8 weeks, a rent rebate of £1.60 is granted. The share of the rent attributed to Harold remains a quarter of the full rent, i.e. £1·50. Mr A.'s supplementary allowance is reduced by the amount of the rent rebate, from £3·30 to £1·70. See page 41.

EXAMPLE B

Mrs B. is a widow aged 45 with a daughter, Judith (17), at school, for whom she receives an education maintenance allowance. She gets a widowed mother's allowance of £10·05 a week and is repaying a mortgage on her house at the rate of £8 a week, £5 of which represents interest. Her father pays her £3 a week to enable her to keep up the capital repayments. The house has a rateable value of £70. Mrs B. has been in receipt of supplementary benefit for over two years and therefore qualifies for the long-term addition of 60p. She is diabetic and needs a special diet.

Requirements			*See page*
Mrs B.		£6·55	
Judy		4·05	
Allowance for 'rent':			
Mortgage interest	£5·00		50
Rates	77		
Repairs and insurance (£13 a year)	25		49
		6·02	
Long-term addition		60	36
Exceptional circumstances:			
Special diet	92		76
Less long-term addition (part available to meet exceptional needs)	50		82–3
		42	
		17·64	
Resources			
Widowed mother's allowance	10·05		
Less disregard	38		64
		9·67	
		7·97	

Supplementary allowance (rounded to nearest 5p)   £7·95

Note: Both the education maintenance allowance and the allowance from Mrs B.'s father are disregarded on a discretionary basis. See page 66.

EXAMPLE C

David C., aged 16, pays his parents £3·50 a week for board and lodging. He is unemployed but has not paid enough insurance contributions to qualify for unemployment benefit.

Requirements		*See page*
David C.	£4·05	} 61
Rent allowance (non-householder)	70	
	4·75	
Resources	Nil	
Supplementary allowance	£4·75	

EXAMPLE D

Miss Mary D., aged 80, lives in a guest house, paying £10·50 a week for board and lodging. The Supplementary Benefits Commission is prepared to meet only £7 of this charge. Miss D. pays the rest out of her savings, which now amount to £1,500. She has an old person's pension of £4·05.

Requirements				*See page*
Board and lodging			£7·00	} 58–60
Personal expenses			2·10	
			9·10	
Resources				
Old person's pension		£4·05		
Assumed income from				
capital	4·50			67–8
Less disregard	1·00			64
		3·50		
			7·55	
Supplementary pension			£1·55	

Note: Miss D. does not qualify for the long-term addition of 85p for a person aged 80 or over, because she is paying an inclusive charge for board and lodging. See page 36.

EXAMPLE E

Edward E. has been on strike for two weeks. His wife does a part-time job, earning £3·10 a week net. They have three children, aged 5, 7, and 8, and pay £5·22 a week rent and rates. Their combined savings are under £325. In the second week of the strike, Edward E. gets a tax refund of £2·80.

Requirements (wife and children only)			*See page*
Mrs E.		£5·20	127
Children – 3 × £2·25		6·75	
Rent and rates		5·22	
		17·17	

Resources				
Mrs E. – earnings	£3·10			
Less disregard	2·00			64–5
		£1·10		
Mr E. – tax refund	2·80			} 129
Less disregard	1·00			
		1·80		
Family allowances		1·90		
Assumed income from capital		Nil		67
		4·80		
		12·37		

Supplementary allowance (rounded to nearest 5p) £12·35

Appendix 3

FORM B/O.40: GUIDE TO ADEQUACY OF CLOTHING STOCKS

overleaf

(1) Articles and standard quantity	*(2) Stocks held	(3) No	(4) £	Cost

Men's garments

Overcoat or raincoat § (1)				
Jacket (1)				
Trousers (2 pairs)				
Waistcoat or sweater (1)				
Socks (3 pairs)				
Boots or shoes (2 pairs)				
Shirts (2)				
Under-vests (2)				
Under-pants (2) (if used)				
Nightshirts or pyjamas (2) (if used) ...				

Women's garments

Overcoat or raincoat § (1).				
Cardigan or jacket (1)				
Dresses ‡ (2)				
Stockings (3 pairs)				
Shoes (2 pairs)				
Petticoats (underslips or underskirts) (2) ...				
Vests (2)				
Knickers (2)				
Brassieres (2) (if used)				
Corsets (1) (if used)				
Nightdresses (2)				

Boys' garments

Overcoat or raincoat § (1)				
Jacket or windcheater (1)				
Trousers (2 pairs)				
Sweater (1)				
Socks or stockings (3 pairs)				
Boots or shoes (2 pairs)				
Shirts (2)				
Under-vests (2)				
Under-pants (2) (if used)				
Nightshirts or pyjamas (2)				

Girls' garments

Overcoat or raincoat § (1)				
Cardigan or jacket (1)				
Dresses ‡ (2)				
Socks or stockings (3 pairs)				
Shoes (2 pairs)				
Petticoats (underslips or underskirts) (2) ...				
Vests (2)				
Knickers (2)				
Corsets (1) (if used)				
Nightdresses (2)				

Bedding

Blankets † (3 per bed in use)				
Sheets (3 per bed in use) ·				
Pillow (1 per person)				
Pillow cases (2 per person)				

Other essential household equipment (Specify deficiencies)..				

* Enter the number of serviceable articles in wear or in use. If no serviceable articles are held or no articles at all are held enter "NONE".
† or two blankets and an eiderdown.
‡ A jumper and skirt count as one dress.
§ As seems appropriate.

Total Amnt		

INDEX

INDEX

MORE ABOUT PENGUINS
AND PELICANS

Penguinews, which appears every month, contains details of all the new books issued by Penguins as they are published. From time to time it is supplemented by *Penguins in Print*, which is a complete list of all available books published by Penguins. (There are well over three thousand of these.)

A specimen copy of *Penguinews* will be sent to you free on request, and you can become a subscriber for the price of the postage. For a year's issues (including the complete lists) please send 30p if you live in the United Kingdom, or 60p if you live elsewhere. Just write to Dept EP, Penguin Books Ltd, Harmondsworth, Middlesex, enclosing a cheque or postal order, and your name will be added to the mailing list.

Note: *Penguinews* and *Penguins in Print* are not available in the U.S.A. or Canada

BRITISH CAPITALISM, WORKERS AND THE PROFITS SQUEEZE

Andrew Glyn and Bob Sutcliffe

According to the authors of this provocative Penguin Special, British capitalism has in the last few years given the lie to the basic assumption of the great majority of Western economists. Work-force's share of the economic cake, like that of Profit, remains more or less constant. They see the implications to be revolutionary, in a literal sense.

They analyse the situation as follows. Because of increasing international competition, firms have been unable to pass on as higher prices the increased wages they have been forced to concede. Profit margins have narrowed. The evidence is clear and plentiful. But without profit to finance dividends and reinvestment, capitalism cannot survive. So which will be sacrificed – the System itself or the prosperity of ninety per cent of the population? Either way the political consequences will be formidable.

A Penguin Special

FREEDOM, THE INDIVIDUAL
AND THE LAW

Harry Street

Civil Liberties are very much in the news. At the heart
of every incident that concerns the rights and
obligations of the individual lies a conflict, sometimes
muted, sometimes violent, between competing
interests: freedom of speech v. security of the state,
freedom of movement v. public order, the right to
privacy v. the demands of a vigilant press. Every day
brings fresh reports of 'punch-up' politics, banning of
controversial posters, curious corners of theatre
censorship, abuse of telephone tapping, contempt of
Parliament . . . the headlines never stop.

Yet Professor Street's *Freedom, the Individual and the Law*
is the first comprehensive survey of the way English
law deals with the many sides of Civil Liberty. After an
introductory description of the powers of the police,
Professor Street addresses himself in detail to the main
areas of freedom of expression, freedom of association,
and freedom of movement. Protection against private
power, the right to work, and other subjects of
contemporary importance make up the citizen's first
guide to the theory and practice of Civil Liberty.

A Pelican Original

THE MANAGEMENT OF GOVERNMENT

John Garrett

The Civil Service, commonly considered overstaffed, inefficient and sluggish, provides an easy scapegoat for multifarious British grievances. Nevertheless, it is required to implement entirely new policies and cope with the creation and dissolution of substantial organizations at very short notice and with no break in continuity. This it achieves 'as effectively as any industry', argues John Garrett, who was a member of the consultancy group employed by the Fulton Committee to examine the Civil Service in 1966.

But intuitive guesswork still takes the place of specialist knowledge on too many occasions. In *The Management of Government* John Garrett thoroughly explores the workings of a labyrinthine institution, with an expert analysis of the areas in which modern management techniques could bring about improvement. He examines the dissatisfaction that led to management reform in the Civil Service, takes a critical look at the Fulton Report, and assesses recent developments in organization, systems of planning, accountability, personnel management, and the 'quiet revolution' promised by the present government.

A Pelican Original

CIVIL LIBERTY
THE NCCL GUIDE

Anna Coote and Lawrence Grant

No constitution or charter protects British rights. At the mercy of any piece of hasty or prejudiced legislation, they must be upheld in every generation.

Do you possess the 'eternal vigilance' required to safeguard liberty? Do you know, for instance, what your rights are if you are arrested or need legal aid; if you are discriminated against or evicted; if you want to cancel a hire purchase agreement or make a complaint against your doctor; if you are getting a divorce or adopting a baby; if you hold a public meeting or go on strike?

If you are unsure, this Penguin Special will supply the answers. You will find detailed here all those questions of liberty, justice and human rights about which most men in the street are ignorant, or, at best, doubtful. In effect this well ordered and useful guide distils the long experience of the National Council for Civil Liberties in standing up (both politically and through case-work) for 'us' against 'them'.

A Penguin Special